CW00832537

YOUNG
CARL JUNG

YOUNG CARL JUNG

Robert W. Brockway

CHIRON PUBLICATION • WILMETTE, ILLINOIS

© 1996 by Chiron Publications. All rights reserved. No part of this publication may be reproduced, stored in a retrieval system, or transmitted, in any form by any means, electronic, mechanical, photocopying, or otherwise, without the prior written permission of the publisher, Chiron Publications, 400 Linden Avenue, Wilmette, Illinois 60091.

Grateful acknowledgment is made for the following permissions:

Diagram, p. 22, is from Jung, C. G., *Analytical Psychology: Notes on the Seminar Given in 1925*. Copyright © 1989 by Princeton University Press. Reprinted/reproduced by permission of Princeton University Press.

Memories, Dreams, Reflections by C. G. Jung, trans. Richard and Clara Winston. Translation copyright © 1961, 1962, 1963, renewed 1989, 1990, 1991 by Random House, Inc. Excerpts reprinted by permission of Pantheon Books, a division of Random House, Inc.

Library of Congress Catalog Card Number: 96-25223

Printed in the United States of America.
Copyedited by Carla Babrick.
Book design by Elaine Hill.
Cover design by D. J. Hyde.

Library of Congress Cataloging-in-Publication Data:

Brockway, Robert W., 1923–
    Young Carl Jung / Robert W. Brockway.
    p.   cm.
    Includes bibliographical references and index.
    ISBN 1-888602-01-5 (pbk.)
    1. Jung, C. G. (Carl Gustav), 1875–1961.   2. Psychoanalysts—
Switzerland—Biography.   3. Jungian psychology.   I. Title.
BF109.J8B73   1996
    150.19′54′092—dc20
    [B]   96–25223
                                                                CIP

ISBN 1–888602–01–5

To Ed, Bob, Peter, Susan,
and Laurie, my friends and
colleagues in the Brandon University
Department of Religion

Author's Note

As I am a naturalized Canadian of American origins, who has lived and taught in England, I have personal preferences in matters of spelling, capitalization, and use of hyphens that conflict with present-day American usage. While I have conformed to *The Chicago Manual of Style and Merriam Webster's Collegiate Dictionary*, Tenth Edition (1994), in deference to my American publisher, I prefer the older British forms on literary and aesthetic grounds. I have C. G. Jung's antipathy for much that is modern.

Robert W. Brockway

Contents

Preface

I am grateful to Franz Jung and Aniela Jaffé, whom I interviewed, as well as to other Swiss such as the archivists of Basel University and Basel Stadt. Many thanks to Dr. Klaus Anton and the Reverend Barbara Anton-Stuwe of Klein-Hüningen. Many thanks as well to the librarian of the C. G. Jung Institute of New York and to Alice Brancewicz of the library services of Brandon University. I wish to thank Dr. Peter Hordern, former dean of the Faculty of Arts, for making research funds available, and to Dr. Robert Florida, the present dean, for continued encouragement. Many thanks to the research committee of Brandon University for research funding. I am also very grateful to my colleagues in the Religion Department: Dr. Edward Milton, Chairman, Dr. Robert Florida, Dr. Peter Hordern, Dr. Laurence Nixon, and Professor Susan Medd. Many thanks to Arts Faculty secretaries Maxine Sobkow, Annelie Baerg, and Janice Mahoney at Brandon University. Many thanks to Chiron Publications editors Murray Stein, Ph.D., and Diane McComb who have made this book possible. Deeper gratitude than I can express to my wife and my best friend, Katie, who, as copy editor, is my collaborator. Finally, my gratitude to our Shetland sheepdog Little Guy just for being.

Prologue

Jung's Last Years

In 1956, Carl Gustav Jung was eighty-one. He had entered a decade in life which few reach, and which nearly all who do find bleak. He was frail and tired easily. He was bereaved because of the loss of his wife Emma the year before (Wehr 1988, 422f.). He also felt alienated from the modern age. He was more famous than he ever had been, and was held in the highest esteem. Yet his lifelong self-doubts remained.

Seeking solitude, Jung habitually spent one week each month at Bollingen, a hamlet on Lake Zürich where he had built a stone tower during the 1920s. Bollingen was Jung's retreat from the twentieth-century world. Born in 1875, he was twenty-five in 1900, and had therefore spent his formative years in the nineteenth century. At Bollingen he lived as he had in his childhood, close to nature and among people who farmed and fished.

When I visited Bollingen, none of the waitresses at the shore café had heard of Jung; neither had the headwaiter at the Laufen restaurant when I visited the Falls of the Rhine. Many people in Küsnacht, his hometown, never have heard of him. There is no portrait of him in the Basel Municipal Museum, no statue or memorial to him in Zürich. Most Swiss seem to be unaware of him. I think that it is safe to say that Jung is far better known in Britain and North America than in continental Europe, even in Switzerland. Indeed, as I was taking my leave after my visit with her, Aniela Jaffé ruefully said, "The prophet is not without honor save in his own country."

A farmer at Bollingen *had* heard of Jung. He pointed out the path that led past his stone tower. I missed it and had to ask directions again. On the way, I met a Swiss couple who were also looking for it and, together, we finally found it, nestling in the woods near the shore. It is much smaller than I had expected from photographs.

Although I have never been in the tower, I know that it is rustic, with a large open fireplace, and with no modern power or conveniences. Here, Jung lived simply without electric lights, modern stove, or refrigerator, but as people did in the days of his childhood. At Bollingen he was attuned to the subtle forces of nature. Bollingen was Jung's Walden, and, in his revulsion against modern technology coupled with a love of nature, he shared much with Henry David Thoreau. At Bollingen Jung lived a simple life, working wood and stone with tools, and cooking over the open hearth. He was a splendid chef. At Bollingen he retreated from the many demands that the world made on him at home.

He was a true Renaissance man: physician, scientist, scholar, craftsman, artist, and athlete. He excelled at all of them. Jung always threw himself completely into whatever he did, whether it was writing a book, clinical work with patients, sailing his boat on the lake, stone masonry, wood carving, mountain climbing, or cuisine. Indeed, Jung built much of the Bollingen tower himself, winning praise from the stone masons he hired to help him.

Although he sometimes called himself "a modern man," Jung was actually a reactionary who felt that he had been born a century too late. When he was twelve he sometimes wrote "1786" instead of "1886" because he wished that he lived in the eighteenth century. He fancied himself as a wise old man wearing a tricorn hat and knee breeches, who had buckles on his shoes and rode in an elegant carriage driven by a brace of spirited white horses (Jung 1961, 34f.). In his late years, he still preferred archaic technology and therefore had no twentieth-century gadgets or conveniences in his tower. Here he lived as he had in the world of his childhood, close to nature, enjoying the stillness of night, the rustle of wind in grass and trees, unhurried days spent in deep thought as he worked in wood and stone with simple tools. He cooked with old-fashioned utensils over the open hearth, yet prepared gourmet meals that are still remembered by former dinner guests like Marie-Louise von Franz.

His retreats to Bollingen were also regressions to the inner world of his rustic childhood. As a boy he had loved to ramble through the Black Forest and Jura Mountains, and, though as sociable and mischievous as any peasant boy in Klein-Hüningen, he particularly cherished the solitary hours of fantasy play when he carved a little manikin from the end of his ruler and hid him in the attic with a stone from the Rhine in a yellow pencil box, or when he was a builder of miniature towns made of stone. At Bollingen, the elderly Jung communed with the deeply buried boy that he had been many decades ago by re-creating the world that had been. At Bollingen he kindled fire, carved wood, shaped stone, and lost himself in thought all the while as he delved into the innermost depths of his mind. He thus engaged himself continually in his *nekya* or "night-sea journey," a word he took from Homer's *Odyssey*. In his terms, it refers to the *descensus ad inferos* (descent into the depths).

Jung's inner explorations of the unconscious lay at the heart of his mythic vision of reality. He classed himself as an *introvert*, a term which he invented, along with *extravert*, which is its opposite. The two terms appeared first in *Psychological Types* (1921). The introvert, among other traits, is aloof, feels lost in crowds, and is inward-looking and reflective. Jung had these qualities. However, he was also frequently very sociable and outgoing, enjoyed making a show of himself, and had a strongly altruistic side, which is typical of the extravert. (Many of the other descriptors of both the extravert and introvert he lists do not, of course, apply to him.) Was he the introvert he claimed to be? He certainly was very complex. Early in his boyhood he became aware of an alternate personality in himself, which he called Personality Number Two (obviously the introvert). Since he was fully aware of this other personality, it was not a case of dissociation. Instead, it was as if two brothers who were as unalike as yin and yang in Chinese thought shared the same body . In later life, these two personalities occupied two geographical locations: Personality Number One in Küsnacht, and Personality Number Two in Bollingen.

At Bollingen, Jung withdrew into himself and became

contemplative and highly subjective. Here, the introverted brother came into his own. The lakeshore village of Bollingen lies east of the little suburban town of Küsnacht on the shore of Lake Zürich. At Küsnacht, Jung was the paterfamilias, visited with his many friends and acquaintances, and was happily engaged in social life. There were always houseguests. Jung enjoyed mingling with people at Küsnacht, and, in his young and middle years, was sometimes a "party animal." He was famous for his hearty laugh. His wife Emma, however, was shy at parties, quiet and withdrawn. She really was an introvert, by Jung's definition, no matter where she was.

The Jungs built a mansion at Küsnacht in 1909 with Emma's money. Küsnacht-Zürich, to give the town its full name, is a fifteen-minute ride east from the Central Station in the heart of Zürich, using one of the swift, electric, interurban trains for which Switzerland is famous. The Jungs spent most of their lives there. His wife Emma died in 1955, and Carl himself in 1961. His octogenarian son Franz lived there until his death in 1996.

My visit to Jung's home at 228 Seestrasse was an unforgettable experience. To be in the house is to grasp the reality of Jung, who has become almost a mythical being in some quarters. It added more to my understanding of Jung than anything I ever have read about him.

Küsnacht-Zürich is a pleasant suburb. The hills which rise behind it slope down to the lakeshore. The village is all residential, with a mix of modest and elegant homes. Seestrasse is a quiet road, which skirts the lake about ten minutes' walk from the little railroad station. The Jung Institute, founded in 1947, is also on Seestrasse, not far from number 228. The mansion the Jungs built during the summer of 1909 is a tall, two-story brick house set in wide grounds. A walk leads to the entrance over which is Jung's motto, *Vocatus atque non vocatus, deus aderit* (called or not called, the god will be there) from Virgil's *Aeneid*.

Franz Jung and his friendly airdale greeted me at the door and ushered me into the high-ceilinged parlor. There, light streams through generous windows. The decor is turn-of-the-century, tasteful, and distinctively European. The most conspicuous feature is the library, which occupies an entire wall to the left. It reaches to the ceiling; the upper shelves are reached with a mobile library-ladder. More books are shelved in the adjoining consulting room where Jung saw his patients. From what I could see, and also from a catalog of the library published by von Franz, most of Jung's books are either classics or studies of religion and myth of the first three decades of the twentieth century. The library says much about Jung's mind and interests.

The Jungs made only the one move, from Burghölzli, where they lived in quarters at the mental hospital after their marriage in February 1903, to Küsnacht, where Jung went into private practice during the summer of 1909. The house in Küsnacht was his contact point with the world. Here he saw his patients, consulted with his colleagues, and socialized with his friends. There were always houseguests, frequent visitors, and, as Jung grew older, he sometimes ruefully complained that he had become a Swiss tourist attraction like the bears of Berne.

In Küsnacht Jung also enjoyed quiet conversations with his closest friends, the inner circle. In his last years, he loved to sit outside on warm summer days, carving wood while he chatted with his intimates. They included Ruth Bailey, a devoted Englishwoman, who took charge of the household after Emma's death, Laurens Van der Post, Jung's South African friend, and women followers who were cheekily called the "Jungfrauen." Jung was very fond of women and felt at ease among them. In his last years his women friends were former patients whom he had later trained as analysts. They included Barbara Hannah, Maria-Louise von Franz, and his part-time secretary, Aniela Jaffé. In 1944, at age sixty-nine, Jung suffered a serious heart attack, and thereafter, his formerly robust health declined. The long-term effects of amoebic dysentery contracted in India in 1938 took their toll as well. Jung endured his infirmities stoically, but they were hard to bear because he had been a very active man. He had to give up mountain climbing and other physical pleasures; when he was in his early eighties, he could walk only a short way without becoming tired. Yet his mind remained remarkably alert and he continued to work.

The elderly Jung was highly productive. In 1955 he brought out *Mysterium Coniunctionis* (volume 14 of *Collected*

Works), his last major work. His mind was churning with other projects as well. He produced papers on synchronicity, his last great idea, and he continued to revise the concept of the psychoid archetype. He was fascinated with UFOs and produced papers on them. He collaborated in the editing of the eighteen volumes of his *Collected Works*, which were completed and published posthumously. It was a time of fulfillment and accomplishment.

It was also a time of grief. In November 1955, Emma died. Jung coped with bereavement by retreating to Bollingen during the winter of 1955–56, one of the harshest on record. "The close of her life," he wrote a correspondent, "the end, and what it made me realize, wrenched me violently out of myself. It cost me a great deal to regain my footing, and contact with stone helped me" (Wehr 1988, 425). He meant his stone carving.

During his last years, his routine was to spend three weeks of every month at Küsnacht and one at Bollingen. He could still sail, and his way to Bollingen from Küsnacht was often by sailboat. Another pleasure was being driven through the countryside, and especially in the mountainous canton of Grisons.

Jung devoted these years mainly to his correspondence, which was voluminous. He answered most of his mail. The letters were collected and published in 1974 in two fat volumes. They are primary sources for Jung's views on religion, the esoteric and occult, myth, and mysticism. In his scientific papers, Jung was objective. Except for the controversial "Answer to Job," (in volume 11 of *Collected Works*), there is little discussion of his personal religious ideas, for example. The letters to clergymen are particularly important because here Jung disclosed his religious views in detail and with considerable frankness. The reader soon discovers that Jung was a mystic, but also that he compartmentalized his personal religiosity away from his scientific concepts and his social and cultural analyses.

In 1959, John Freeman of the BBC persuaded Jung to participate in the writing of *Man and His Symbols*, a nontechnical book addressed to the general public. Jung was to write the first chapter himself and to approve others written by von Franz, Jaffé, Jolande Jacoby, and Joseph Henderson. He was busy on "Approaching the Unconscious" during his last months, finishing it just ten days before the onset of his final illness.

The night before he died, while housekeeper Ruth Bailey was occupied elsewhere, the ailing Jung had his son Franz help him out of bed and to the window for one last look at his beloved Alps in glowing sunset red. As a child of three and a half, he had been shown them by an aunt and had been awestruck by their beauty. He died the next afternoon. That night there was a tremendous thunderstorm and a bolt of lightning shattered one of his favorite trees.

In 1964, *Errinerungen, Träume, Gedanken* appeared, which Richard and Clara Winston translated as *Memories, Dreams, Reflections*. It was mostly written by Aniela Jaffé from interviews with Jung. The first three chapters, those dealing with his early years, school days, and university years, were written by Jung himself in his own hand. He also wrote "Late Thoughts," the last chapter. Of the other chapters, that dealing with his apprentice years at Burghölzli seems to have been of composite authorship. "Confrontation with the Unconscious," the most important of the chapters in my opinion, was adapted from notes from a special seminar on analytical psychology of the year 1925, in which Jung explained the origin of his concepts in sixteen lectures. The notes have been recently published. Those dealing with Jung's travels were based on papers he wrote on the Pueblo Indians and the Elgonyi of East Africa, as well as other travel notes.

What do we know about Jung's early years? Very little. Born on May 26, 1875, in the parsonage of Kesswil, a village near Lake Constance, Carl Gustav Jung was taken by his young parents to Laufen at Rhinefall. In 1879 or 1880, his father, the Reverend Johann Paul Achilles Jung, Ph.D. (1842–96) and his mother Emilie, née Preiswerk (1848–1923), moved to the village of Klein-Hüningen across the Rhine from Basel. We know this much about Jung's childhood from the city records of Basel, of which his parents were citizens. We also have a few anecdotes supplied in 1935 by a boyhood friend of Jung's, Albert Oeri. We know from Oeri that at age four Carl Gustav was a very rude host who completely ignored Albert when his parents brought him for a visit. Oeri also mentioned a few of Jung's pranks when he was nine or ten.

Almost everything else is conjecture based on *Errinerungen, Träume, Gedanken* (*Memories, Dreams, Reflections*), finished when he was eighty-three. Scholars continue to argue about this remarkable book which, Jung claimed, was his "story of the self-realization of the unconscious," his "myth." "Whether or not the stories are 'true' is not the problem," he wrote. It is rather his inward vision, *sub specie aeternitatis* (Jung 1961, 3).

When I asked Jaffé about Jung's childhood, she gently chided me for being Freudian. In this respect, she was not wrong. I think that childhood plays an enormous role in forming and determining psychological life and that few people, if any, entirely grow up. From that point of view, the lack of interest in child psychology on Jung's part, and among Jungians generally, always has puzzled me. However, in his own case, Jung attributed his discovery of the collective unconscious to early childhood experiences beginning with a particularly vivid dream of an underground, castle-like chamber, in which he saw a giant, enthroned, erect penis. This dream, which haunted him throughout life, seems to have played an important role in his discovery of the collective unconscious. In his later reflections, he could not explain the dream by anything in his life experience as a four-year-old. The dream was therefore the centerpiece of his work.

As previously mentioned, Jung classed himself as an introvert, a personality type which, in his theory of personality, is self-stimulating, inward-looking, and self-preoccupied, but quite capable at times of being sociable, outgoing, and concerned with other people. The only child is often an introvert, and Jung was an only child until the age of nine. In some ways, he continued to be so after the birth of his sister Gertrude because there was such a wide gap in their ages. In actuality, Paul and Emilie Jung reared two only children serially.

Comparatively little attention has been given only children in psychological literature, and, for that reason, my own experience as an only child has helped me to understand Jung. The first time I read the opening chapters of *Memories, Dreams, Reflections*, I sensed a fellow spirit. As Joseph Campbell once said, the introvert is always asking himself, "How am I doing?"

Even in old age, the typical introvert recalls early intuitions, dreams, inner thoughts, solitary games, and fantasies much more vividly than the outer events of life and the people he or she knew. This is certainly true in my own case, and I think that it was true of Jung. Like cats, introverts are more attached to places than to people. To them, people are problems. Introverts may adjust well to social demands, but always prefer the world of nature or of the city to its human inhabitants. Contrary to popular notions, introverts are frequently very sociable and convivial. But this is persona; it is protective covering. The introvert is much more interested in his or her own inner life. He or she is seldom bored by a rainy day. He or she does not need external stimulation. Instead, his or her mind is constantly preoccupied with images, visions, and ideas which tumble, doing somersaults like clowns.

Paul Stern, in *C. G. Jung: The Haunted Prophet* (1979), accuses Jung of being a narcissist, as does Peter Homans in *Jung in Context: Modernity and the Making of a Psychology* (1979). Is this charge sound? Jung's admirers do not deny his introversion, nor did Jung himself. To some, this is egoism, and therefore reprehensible. Introverts, however, interpret the very same phenomenon as depth of thought and feeling, and they accuse extraverts of being both superficial and overly dependent on outside stimulation. It is, in other words, a subjective value judgment as to which personality type is preferable.

When he was in school, Carl, though very sociable, had typically introvertish problems in interpersonal relations. He had trouble understanding the motives of others. As is true of many introverts, people baffled him, and, like many in his field, he probably became a psychologist on that account. Even in old age, he preferred the solitude of Bollingen. He is quite frank in *Memories* concerning occasions on which he was cold and unfeeling, as when he was clinically fascinated with his father's death throes. Jung's self-acknowledged introversion is constantly evidenced in the chapter "School Years." Anyone who was an only child immediately recognizes the fantasies and inner preoccupations. Whether these are pathological, antisocial, or unfeeling is another matter.

The Writing of *Memories, Dreams, Reflections*

Both the original German text of *Memories, Dreams, Reflections* and the English translation by Richard and Clara Winston were published soon after Jung's death on June 6, 1961. In some ways, it is the most important of his works, certainly among the most controversial. Now, more than thirty years after the appearance of *Memories, Dreams, Reflections*, it continues to be analyzed and debated. The most recent discussion is Richard Noll's *The Jung Cult: Origins of a Charismatic Movement* (1994), to which I will soon turn. But first, a word should be said about the writing of Jung's autobiography.

During the later years of his life, friends and correspondents often had tried to persuade Jung to write a memoir or an autobiography, and he had always refused. He did not have a high opinion of autobiographies because he considered them full of lies and evasions, and he also did not think that writing one was an appropriate way for him to spend whatever time he had left (Jung 1961, viii).

After Jung turned eighty, the suggestions that he write an autobiography became more urgent and insistent. Among those interested was the German-American publisher Kurt Wolff, who had escaped Hitler's Germany in 1941. He settled in New York, where he became director of Pantheon Books. In Germany, he had been one of the progressively minded publishers who encouraged expressionistic poets and other avant-garde writers. In America, his interest in Jung was roused by Mary and Paul Mellon, two wealthy philanthropists who knew Jung well.

In August 1956, Wolff attended the Eranos conference, where he urged Jung's friends to try to persuade Jung to write his autobiography. Jaffé had just become Jung's secretary the year before, and, on Jacoby's suggestion, she was elected to talk Jung into it.

Jaffé was the best person to persuade Jung to do an autobiography; she was closest to Jung and understood him well. However, she was not optimistic. Jung always had refused, and two years before, wrote to an old friend, Henri Flournoy, that he distrusted autobiography because "We never tell the truth about ourselves." He added "I am almost seventy-eight which Cicero would have called *tempus matura mortis*, (time ripe for death).

In October 1990, I met Frau Jaffé, still a practicing analyst although she was nearly blind, ailing, and eighty-seven when I talked with her in her home in Zürich. She had been a Jewish refugee who fled to Switzerland during the mid-1930s. She arrived destitute. Jung befriended her, helped her settle, found her work. "He was so good to a little Jewish girl," she told me. It still bothered her deeply that Jung was accused of anti-Semitism. She staunchly denied that there was anything to it, and said that his flirtation with the Third Reich during the early 1930s was partly because of political naiveté and partly because he was fascinated with the surfacing of archaic symbols and myths in a modern culture.

Jaffé succeeded where others had failed, and Jung reluctantly agreed after much soul-searching because it might help him in his present work. At the time, Jung was busy with other projects and heavy correspondence. However, he gave an afternoon a week to the project, beginning in the spring of 1957. What was wanted was an autobiography in the first person with Jung as narrator. Jung, who hated modern gadgets, would not have a tape recorder used, and so Jaffé interviewed him question-and-answer fashion. That went slowly, and, at first, Jung was reticent. Then he became more involved and, by the end of the year, "After a period of inner turbulence, long-submerged images out of his childhood rose to the surface of his mind" (Jung 1961, vi). One morning, Jung told Jaffé that he wanted to write about his childhood himself. "By this time he had already told me a good many of his earliest memories," Jaffé recalled, "but there were still great gaps in the story" (ibid.). Jaffé was delighted. Jung wrote three chapters in his own hand, finishing them in April 1958. He first called them "On the Early Events of My Life" and then divided them into three chapters: "First Years," "School Years," and "Student Years."

Jung also wrote the last chapter, "Late Thoughts," in January 1959 at Bollingen. According to Jaffé, "When he returned the chapter, 'On Life after Death,' he said to me, 'Something within me has been touched. A gradient has been formed, and I must write.'" Jung "voiced his deepest and perhaps his most far-reaching convictions" (Jung 1961, vii).

According to Jaffé, Jung finished the first three chapters in April 1957. They tell us little about the external events of his childhood and youth, which he claimed not to remember, but present his octogenarian memories of early thoughts, fantasies, and visions. For that reason, we never know how much is Jung the boy and how much is Jung the old man. We also do not know how much is Jung and how much is the result of editing. The documentary corroboration is limited to a few old photographs, a report card, and two entries from the diary which Jung kept when he was a university student. These are reproduced by Aniela Jaffé in her *C. G. Jung: Word and Image* (1979). Other records have not yet been released by the family.

The four chapters by Jung were edited by Jaffé. It was a collaborative work. In her introduction, Jaffé acknowledges her indebtedness to Helen and Kurt Wolff, Marianne and Walther Niehus-Jung, and R.F.C. Hull, and suggests that there were others involved. According to Noll, mention of Toni Wolff was edited out early in the building of the book because of "objections by members of the Jung family while Jung was a semi-invalid in his last years. The book is therefore a product of discipleship" (Noll 1994, 138).

Richard Noll's Critique

In 1994, Richard Noll's *The Jung Cult: The Origin of a Charismatic Movement* appeared. It is one of the most important commentaries on Jung in recent years. According to Noll, *Memories, Dreams, Reflections* is a "sacralization" of Jung, very much like a religious text. "It is now apparent that like the Gospels, *MDR*, too, seems to be the work of many hands other than Jung's own, casting some doubt on its claim to be an autobiography." Noll compares it with accounts of late antique pre-Christian mystics such as the *theos aner* or "divine man" and the ascetic "holy man."

As evidence, Noll cites Jung's focus on dreams, visions, parapsychological experiences, and, in "Late Thoughts," his near-death experience in 1943. These put Jung's autobiography in the same category as *The Life of Apollonius of Tyana* of Philostrates (third century C.E.) or, to a lesser degree, medieval hagiographies. The autobiography is not "the human history of a renowned physician and scientist" but "the myth of a divine hero, a holy man, a saint, a life produced directly by essentially a *religious* community, and therefore a biography as 'cult legend' " (Noll 1994, 14f.).

These accusations have been made before. In 1976, Paul Stern in *C. G. Jung: The Haunted Prophet* accused Jung of writing a "canny propaganda tract promoting the image of the 'wise old man'. . ." and that *Memories* is "in a sense, a self-conscious gospel and Bible of the Jungian dispensation, in the form of a parable." He called the Jung Institute at Küsnacht Jung's "mystical body." Jung's reasons for writing it, according to Stern, included his lack of faith in "the intellectual and literary gifts of his more devout apostles," and therefore "he decided to lend a helping hand in preparing his own transfiguration" (Stern 1976, 16f.). *Memories, Dreams, Reflections* was therefore composed with ulterior motives in mind, "For he was born into a bleak and harsh world, made endurable only by its transfiguration through myth" (Stern 1976, 20).

Noll argues that *Memories, Dreams, Reflections* is an example of "manufactured pseudocharisma" characteristic of "celebrity biography," which "power-seeking elites" use "to promote seductive fantasy images in order to secure and maintain economic and social rewards." He adds that we must somehow find "pre-Jaffé biographical material" to discover the historical Jung, a task which he compares to attempts to "discern the true pre-Pauline facts concerning Jesus of Nazareth" (Noll 1994, 15).

These charges cannot be dismissed lightly. Indeed, some of the more devout "apostles" of Jung have substantiated some of them by writing hagiography. Of these, Marie-Louise von Franz and Laurens Van der Post have been the most extravagant. Among biographies written by Jungians, Barbara Hannah's *Jung: His Life and Work: A Biographical Memoir* (1976) is much less so. (The same charge of hero worship, incidentally, can be leveled against Ernest Jones, whose three-volume semi-official biography of Sigmund Freud is also hagiography.) On the other hand, Gerhard Wehr's *Jung: A Biography* (1988), though by a disciple, is balanced and scholarly in approach.

A number of scholarly studies of Jung have appeared in recent years which are objective. Several of them are revisions of doctoral dissertations and therefore were subject to intense academic scrutiny during the process of research and writing.

Noll's critique refers to the situation that prevailed during the late 1960s and early 1970s, when *Memories, Dreams, Reflections* appeared, and the writings of Jung's warmest apologists such as those of Jaffé, Van der Post, Jacoby, Hannah, and von Franz were published, to be answered chiefly by Freudian polemicists such as D. Winnicott and Stern.

Contemporary publications about Jung, such as F. X. Charet's *Spiritualism and the Foundations of C. G. Jung's Psychology* (1993) and Robert Aziz's *C. G. Jung's Psychology of Religion and Synchronicity* (1990), are highly objective scholarly analyses. Indeed, in his *The Discovery of the Unconscious* (1970), Henri Ellenberger presented a balanced discussion which in many respects has not been equalled. In his preface and elsewhere, Noll expresses warm appreciation for Ellenberger and, indeed, shows his indebtedness to him.

There is today an anti-Jungian reaction in some quarters comparable to that against Freud during the 1980s, especially when Jeffrey Masson Moussaieff's highly polemical *The Assault on Truth: Freud's Suppression of the Seduction Theory* (1984) appeared. It was intended to demolish Freud and, indeed, did so in some quarters. However, the long-term effect has been that of an appropriate corrective. In my view, the same is true of anti-Jungian polemics in general, and Noll's book in particular.

My surprise is that Noll expects *Memories, Dreams, Reflections* to be historical biography when both Jaffé's introduction and Jung's prologue specifically insist that it is not. Instead, it is exactly what the very apt title should lead us to expect. The book presents Jung's memories, certain dreams, visions, and fantasies that fascinated him, and his subjective thoughts about life, death, and God, which continued to perplex him during his last days. Why should anyone expect it to be an historical biography when all such intentions are expressly denied at the outset? Instead, the reader must accept the book for what it is. As for "pre-Jaffé" data, unless or until the Jung family archives are made available to scholars, we have only what has been released. The recent publication of the Zofingia papers, indeed, suggests that more might be forthcoming someday, but, until then, we have very little "pre-Jaffé" documentation for the early years of Jung's life. For later years, we have the voluminous correspondence, much of which has been published, in addition to the *Collected Works*, and, most recently, *Analytical Psychology: Notes of the Seminar Given in 1925 by C. G. Jung*, edited by William McGuire and published in 1989 (Jung 1925). We also have *The Freud/Jung Letters: The Correspondence Between Sigmund Freud and C. G. Jung* edited by William McGuire (1974). There is, therefore, a great deal of "extra-Jaffé" data now available to scholars, which was not so during the early 1970s when most of the controversial commentaries on *Memories, Dreams, Reflections* appeared.

Few great men and women preserve much documentation from childhood and youth. As mentioned earlier, in Jung's case some of this has been made available by Jaffé in her *C. G. Jung: Word and Image* (1979). Indeed, all of the original manuscript of *Memories, Dreams, Reflections* was apparently not published. There are probably more documents in the Jung family archives. If they ever come to light, we may fill in a few gaps and, in any case, be able to write a historical biography of Jung's childhood and early youth. Curiously, even Jung's closest living relatives seem to know very little about his early years. As it is, we have as much or more about these years as we do for George Washington and Abraham Lincoln, for example. Thanks to *Memories, Dreams, Reflections*, however, we have far more about Jung's inner life as a boy than we do for anyone, except perhaps for the authors of autobiographical novels (e.g., Charles Dickens and his *David Copperfield*). Thanks to the two volumes of *Letters of C. G. Jung* (1906–61), which were published in 1974, and *The Freud/Jung Letters*, we have considerably more data about Jung's mature years than we do for most historical figures.

Noll argues that *Memories, Dreams, Reflections* is a sacred text which arose in a religious community, and that Jung and his followers deliberately intended to found a charismatic cult (Noll 1974, 17). Is the charge just? If so, Jung lied and his associates have been lying about *Memories, Dreams, Reflections* for the past forty years. Jung consistently maintained that he was the only Jungian. He always insisted that he was an empiricist, and that analytic psychology is a science. Those closest to Jung have agreed. Who is right? Was Jung the prophet of a new religion or was he an explorer of the unconscious mind, a psychodynamic psychologist? Did he found a cult or a school of psychology? In my view, while Jung was personally a mystic, as Jaffé readily acknowledges, he regarded his work as empirical research. At the same time, his scientific methodology was flawed, and he was sometimes too dependent on subjective evidence. In that, he was in the good company of scientists such as Charles Darwin, whose *The Descent of Man* (1871) was highly speculative. Perhaps

Jung was a good nineteenth-century scientist who was too late for his time, a generalist in an age of specialization. At any rate, Jung denied having ambitions to found a religious movement. Where some of Jung's followers are concerned, Noll has a strong argument when he calls analytical psychology a charismatic cult. He also has a strong argument when he traces many of Jung's ideas to predecessors such as Ernst Haeckel and other chiefly German-speaking intellectuals of the late nineteenth and early twentieth centuries. I do not agree with the charge, however, that Jung and the Jungians conspired to found a secret cult, and that they have had ulterior motives never expressed in any of their written work nor imparted to students in the institutes.

Noll's charge that *Memories, Dreams, Reflections* is not objective biography is well taken. However, it was not intended to be, as both Jung and Jaffé make clear in their introductory remarks. Except for the notes from the seminar in 1925, it is not based on diaries, journals, notes, or any documents from Jung's past so far as we know. It is admittedly subjective.

Jung quite appropriately wrote in his prologue:

> What we are to our inward vision, and what man appears to be *sub specie aeternitatis*, can only be expressed by way of myth. Myth is more individual and expresses life more precisely than does science. Science works with concepts of averages which are far too general to do justice to the subjective variety of an individual life.
>
> Thus it is that I have now undertaken, in my eighty-third year, to tell my personal myth. I can only make direct statements, only "tell stories." Whether or not the stories are "true" is not the problem. The only question is whether what I tell is *my* fable, *my* truth. (Jung 1961, 3)

Jung is very candid here and in what follows. He warns us that autobiography is "so difficult to write because we possess no standards, no objective foundation, from which to judge ourselves. . . . Like every other being, I am a splinter of the infinite deity." (Jung 1961, 3f.). We therefore have no right to expect historical accuracy as to times, places, or events, just as those to whom we tell personal anecdotes about events in our lives should not expect accuracy. We do, however, have the right to expect honesty. Do we have it?

Here we have an insoluble problem because the answer depends on knowing Jung's mind. There are, however, some helpful indications in his behavior and that of the Jungians.

In her introduction to the work, Jaffé describes in some detail the way it was written. Jung read through and approved the manuscript. "Occasionally he corrected passages or added new material. In turn, I have used the records of our conversations to supplement the chapters he wrote himself, have expanded his sometimes terse allusions, and have eliminated repetitions. The further the book progressed, the closer became the fusion between his work and mine" (Jung 1961, vii). This point is important in view of the charges made by Stern, and recently by Noll, that Jung's autobiography is composite in origin, and that this, in some way, detracts from it. Far from denying the collective origins of the work, Jaffé freely admitted it in her introduction. Jaffé tells us that "the chapters are rapidly moving beams of light that only fleetingly illuminate the outward events of Jung's life and work. In recompense, they transmit the atmosphere of his intellectual world and the experience of a man to whom the psyche was a profound reality" (Jung 1961, vii). She speaks of the casual, conversational tone of the autobiography, and frequently reiterates that it is not an ordinary biography. Jaffé often asked for details about the outer events of his life, but in vain. Only the spiritual essence of his life's experience remained in his memory, and this alone seemed to him worth the effort of telling. Jung, in his memories, visions, and reflections recaptured his inner childhood world again as an octogenarian. He inwardly returned to what he had been.

Jung's World

An important facet of anyone's biography is the geographical and social environment of one's early years. We are all products of the world around us and of the past, both our personal past and the historical past. This is so obvious that it scarcely needs emphasis. Yet it is often forgotten.

Jung spent his boyhood in Swiss Rhenish villages, and especially Klein-Hüningen, across the Rhine from Basel. This was his boyhood world. As Miss Marple constantly tells us in Agatha Christie's mysteries, one can learn everything there is to know about human nature in a village.

While Jung did not subscribe to German political ideals, he was German in culture. His ideas emerged, in part, from the late nineteenth-century context of German thought and from fin de siècle intellectual movements such as *Naturphilosophie*, vitalism, neo-Kantianism, the Dionysian visions of Friedrich Nietzsche, esotericism, Spiritualism, and, above all, the phenomenon which George Mosse and Richard Noll refer to as *Völkischness*. All of these various movements and others are late nineteenth-century currents flowing from German romanticism.

This is not to say, as does Noll, that analytical psychology is a form of German romanticism, vitalism, neo-Kantianism, *Völkischness*, the fin de siècle, or any other specific German intellectual movement of the late nineteenth century. Rather, these and other forces were the cultural context of his formative years so he was inevitably affected by them. Though Swiss in nationality and citizenship, Jung was a German in culture. His memoir is that of a European who grew up during the last quarter of the nineteenth century and who was profoundly affected by the Germanic culture of that era.

Memories, Dreams, Reflections is neither a biography as that term is usually meant, nor a cultic text like Madame Helena Blavatsky's *Isis Unveiled* or Mary Baker Eddy's *Science and Health*. Instead, as discussed previously, it is an interior journey like the *Confessions* of Augustine or those of Rousseau. In some quarters, it has been misused as a quasi-religious text by enthusiastic devotees. I do not, however, believe that this was Jung's intention, Stern and Noll to the contrary. Jung calls it a myth, and, I think rightly so if, by *myth*, one means "story." In many ways it is a psychological novel like Virginia Woolf's *To the Lighthouse*, James Joyce's *Ulysses*, or Christopher Isherwood's *Berlin Stories*. With such novels it is impossible to know fact from fiction, even though the persona is the author himself. It is also impossible to know what is Jung and what is Jaffé. The problem is somewhat the same as with Socrates. How much is Socrates and how much is Plato? We know something about the childhood impressions, fantasies, and dreams of Jung, but little that we can be certain of concerning his life.

What do we know of him? Perhaps, as with Sophocles and Shakespeare, we know something of his mind even though we know almost nothing that is reliable about his early years. The least that can be said is that we know what he thought about his early years when he was in his early eighties. We have his memories, which include recollection of early reflections and dreams. Just as we cannot go behind the gospels to the historical Jesus, so we cannot go behind *Memories, Dreams, Reflections* to the historical Jung. I agree with Noll about what he calls the "quest for the historical Jung," with Albert Schweitzer's *The Quest for the Historical Jesus* (1907) in mind. The analogy, which is a good one, also applies to the inner fellowship of Jungians and especially to the Jungfrauen. When Jaffé told me that her life purpose had been to be Jung's secretary, she might have said that she was his evangelist in the sense of being his gospel writer. Only in his correspondence and in *Memories, Dreams, Reflections* did Jung speak for himself. But what in the memoir is actually from him, and what is the result of his collaboration with her? I am convinced that both were honest. But I agree with Noll that the collaboration undoubtedly affected the memoir. Noll is probably right in saying that the final work, including the editing, made it a collective product, like the books of the New Testament. However, I do not think that there is a Jung cult, that *Memories, Dreams, Reflections* is the word of a "church," or that the inner circle of Jungians deliberately set out to found a Jung cult as an organized religion. At the same time, there are some individual Jungians to whom *Memories, Dreams, Reflections is* a sacred scripture, and who *do* attempt to make a personal religion of Jungian concepts. This approach is particularly true of the New Age. Where that has occurred, it was without his approval, and it is not the intention of the Jung institutes, Jungian analysts, or the view of most people who are attracted to analytical psychology. Precisely because he was an introvert, Jung was not likely to be interested in founding any kind of movement or in assuming any sort of leadership role. This undoubtedly underlay his reluctance to become Freud's "crown prince." He did not want the role. At the same time, he did not want to found a rival movement either. His interest was overwhelmingly in his own inner world and in his ongoing confrontation with the unconscious.

Except for possible lapses of memory and distortions of recall, there is no reason to doubt the anecdotes he mentions in

"School Years." They are all quite believable and consistent. We are, however, on much more dubious grounds with the early dreams and visions, including that of the underground phallus king.

In summary, I think that *Memories, Dreams, Reflections* is actually a literary work, a novel, and that this is what Jung meant when he said that he was writing a "myth." It is an autobiographical novel in which Jung created a character, himself. Similarly, *David Copperfield* is not an authentic biography of Dickens but a work of art. I think that *Memories, Dreams, Reflections* is also a work of art. I say the same of Freud's *Interpretation of Dreams*, which is a revelation of the author's internal journey. Most authorities on creative writing argue that it is impossible to write a completely authentic autobiography because of lapses of memory. The moment that life experience is translated into words, one invents. It is inevitable. By calling his autobiography a myth, Jung acknowledged this fact.

Jung's motive, in my view, was to reveal his experiences of the archetypes of the collective unconscious, and, by so doing, to vindicate his theory. Inner life therefore preoccupied him. The fiery magma of his volcanic metaphor erupts in the dreams, visions, and other psychic experiences of every human being. What he reveals are his personal experiences of an impersonal dimension of psyche. At the same time, *Memories, Dreams, Reflections* is "remembrances of things past." Yet the book is not an exercise in nostalgia because what interests Jung most about his memories are those occasions on which the archetypes emerged into consciousness through symbols and dream images.

One

C. G. Jung's World

The Geology of the Psyche

During the spring and summer of 1925, C. G. Jung presided over a series of sixteen sessions on analytical psychology during a special seminar held in the Psychology Club in Zürich on Wednesday mornings beginning on March 23. The last session was held on July 6. The series was the first formal seminar given by Jung, also the first to have notes recorded and multigraphed. Cary F. De Angulo kept notes which were published in 1989 under the title *Analytical Psychology: Notes of the Seminar Given in 1925 by C. G. Jung* (Jung 1925, xiii). The seminar was for the benefit of English-speaking people. Twenty-seven people attended, of whom thirteen were Americans and six were British (Jung 1925, vii). Jung lectured and responded to questions. In the course of the sessions, he explained how he discovered the collective unconscious. Many years later, he and Aniela Jaffé made De Angulo's notes (Jung 1925, xiii) the basis of chapter 6, "Confrontation with the Unconscious," in *Memories, Dreams, Reflections*.

In the course of his lectures, Jung used ten diagrams to illustrate his concept of the psyche. On July 6, at the close of his last lecture, Jung presented a large colored diagram (shown on page 2) and explained the "geology" of the personality. As he said:

[It] shows individuals coming out of a certain common level, like the summits of mountains coming out of a sea. The first connection between certain individuals is that of the family, then comes the clan which unites a number of families, then the nation which unites a still bigger group. After that we could take a large group of connected nations such as would be included under the heading "European man." Going further down, we would come to what we would call the monkey group, or that of the primate ancestors, and after that would come the animal layer in general, and finally the central fire, with which as the diagram shows, we are still in connection. (Jung 1925, 133f.)

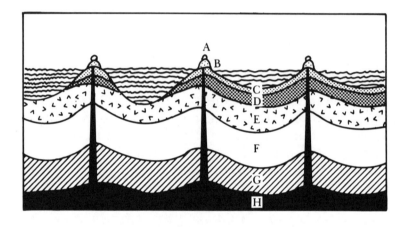

A = Individuals.
B = Families.
C = Clans.
D = Nations.
E = Large Group (European man, for example).
F = Primate Ancestors.
G = Animal Ancestors in general.
H = "Central Fire."

Figure 1

The diagram reminds me of the Hawaiian Islands, where I grew up. The islands are of volcanic origin, each the tip of a submarine mountain in a chain that extends for two thousand miles from the big Island of Hawai'i to tiny Kure atoll beyond Midway. Eight of the islands support complex life-forms including human beings of many racial origins. The deeper one descends into the depths, however, the simpler are the life-forms and also the geological formations. Yet, because fiery magma continues to surge upward through many strata of rock to the active volcanic craters of Kilauea and Mauna Loa on the Island of Hawai'i, the life-forms of the islands are still in connection with the central fire.

In his closing comments in his lecture of July 6, 1925, Jung said that "you must not think of [the collective unconscious] as being compassed by the brain alone but as including the sympathetic nervous system as well." The latter is the inheritance from the primitive invertebrate forms of life. The central nervous system evolved later and is our inheritance from our vertebrate ancestors. It comprises the cerebrospinal system. "The most recent human layers form the basis of actual consciousness, and thus the collective unconscious is reaching into consciousness, and only thus far can you call the collective unconscious psychological." Therefore, most of the collective unconscious is not "psychological" but "psychical." It is "outside" our brains and works on us "through trans-subjective facts which are probably inside as well as outside [ourselves]" (Jung 1925, 131).

In the chart, Jung labeled the lowest and most basic level of the psyche "fiery magma," his metaphor for the life force that also denotes the archetypes of the collective unconscious. In each of the mountains in the chain, magma surges up to the surface. It moves within a channel affected by the strata through which it passes on its upward journey: animal ancestors, early human ancestors, culture, ethnicity, clan, family, and at the summit, the individual. From Jung's viewpoint, therefore, the psyche has various depths and dimensions formed and shaped by biological instinct, race, nationality, clan, and family. Where did Jung get this concept?

In part, it arose from his mature reflection on certain inner experiences that he had from early childhood to the end of his life. Such experiences consisted of dreams, fantasies, and visions that he could not explain in terms of day residue, his personal imagination, or flights of fancy. They happened to him without his having willed them. Some of his dreams, fantasies, and visions, moreover, seemed to have no connection with his personal life. He called these "archetypal" and distinguished them from those he could account for in his conscious, waking life, or those that could be accounted for in terms of what he called the "personal unconscious." The latter is made up of repressed material as well as that which can be accounted for in terms of the individual's life experience.

A third category of psychic experience, which Jung did not always distinguish clearly enough from the archetypes of the collective unconscious, was religious experience. In his scientific writings, Jung did not speak of God or of his personal religious experiences. He did, however, discuss "the God-image in the human psyche" or the "God-archetype" of which the mandala is a symbol. As Jaffé puts it: "In the first case [his religious experiences] he is speaking as an individual, whose thoughts are influenced by passionate, powerful feelings, intuitions, and experiences of a long and unusually rich life." In the second, however, (the God-archetype), he speaks as a scientist (Jung 1961, xi).

Subject and object are not always clear in Jung's writings about religion, most of which are to be found in his correspondence with clergymen in the second volume of his letters. However, when Jung speaks of his passionate, intuitive, religious feelings and also of certain visions, it seems quite clear that these are conscious and do not originate in the collective unconscious, which is ultimately biological. Jung called himself a "radical Protestant," and what he describes as personal religious experiences seems to be very much like that described by William James in *The Varieties of Religious Experience* or in Evelyn Underhill's *Mysticism*.

In 1909, these experiences inspired him to inscribe the lintel of the doorway to his home in Küsnacht-Zürich with the Latin motto *Vocatus atque non vocatus deus aderit* (Called or not called the god will be there). I interpret these experiences as *hierophanies*, to use Mircea Eliade's term, revelations of some modality of the sacred (Eliade 1963, 2). As Jung wrote a young clergyman in 1952: "I find that all my thoughts circle around God like the planets around the sun, and are as irresistibly attracted by Him. I would feel it to be the grossest sin if I were to oppose any resistance to this force" (Jung 1961, xi). This, I would say, is religious experience and, as such, conscious response to what Jung regarded as objective divinity and not an experience that emerged from the collective unconscious.

To add to this confusion, however, Jung attributed his initial discovery of the collective unconscious both to experiences that were psychic and those that he regarded as religious. His concept of the "God-archetype" is the point where they meet. The latter is the divine as we experience it and is, of necessity, the only way that we can experience it: through symbols. Jung denied the possibility of our grasping objective metaphysical realities by any other means. Instead, we only experience them through symbols, myths, and other forms of imagery, which are archetypal and therefore ultimately rooted in the sympathetic nervous system. Yet Jung, as a theist, accepted the objective reality of God as ultimate reality wholly independent of us or any of our concepts, however they may arise. His was the perennial dilemma of the mystic, the subject/object dichotomy that philosophy and theology never have been able to cope with, much less solve. At the same time, in his letters to clergymen, Jung always rejected the terms *faith* and *belief* and, as in his famous BBC interview at the end of his life, always said, "I do not believe, I know."

Memories, Dreams, Reflections is about his inner experiences. Jung's concept of the collective unconscious was inspired chiefly by religious experiences, which began at the age of three and a half with a baffling dream that haunted him throughout his whole life, and that will be discussed later. This was the dream of the underground phallus king, which he could not account for in terms of anything in his life experience as a tiny child. Others, myself included, may disagree with Jung's interpretation, but it must be acknowledged that his reflections on this particular dream were highly important to Jung when he was working out his concept of the collective unconscious during the years between 1912 and 1916. Because we cannot go behind what Jung tells us of the dream to the dream itself, we can only comment on Jung's interpretation of it.

Because Jung did not grow up in a vacuum but in a particular society, the German-Swiss, at a particular time of history, the last two decades of the nineteenth century, his concepts also owe a great deal to the currents and fashions of the German-speaking world of the 1880s and 1890s. Therefore, Jung's world was both his inner realm of private experience and the outer world of Germanic Europe of the late nineteenth century. He cannot be understood apart from this complex subjective and objective context.

Jung's conscious working out of his psychological premises begins, I think, with his personal religious quest. As the son of a Swiss Reformed pastor, Carl was subject to more religious influence than most boys. It has been said, with Nietzsche in mind, that the German *Pfarrhaus* or parsonage has been the spawning ground of German philosophy. There is something to be said for that and it certainly applies to Jung. "Pastor's Carl," as he was nicknamed in his boyhood, encountered the imponderables of life and death in funerals, church services, and the daily lives of his father's parishioners; also in contradictions between religious idealism and reality in the quarrels of his irritable parents, the frustrations of their private lives, and the irrelevance of religious consolation to what affected them most deeply. Therefore, he rejected both church and theology very early without, however, rejecting the realities of religious experience. In turn, religious experience later led him first to parapsychology and then to psychiatry. This was his route to the discovery of the collective unconscious.

When Carl Gustav Jung was a boy of twelve or thirteen, religious doubts led him to pore over the books in his father's small library in quest of God. There he found Biedermann's *Christliche Dogmatik* (1869), which discussed the nature of God as "personality to be conceived after the analogy of the human ego: the uniquely, utterly supermundane ego who embraces the entire cosmos." The idea first intrigued and then repelled him. "I felt the strongest resistances to imagining God by analogy with my own ego," he wrote later in *Memories, Dreams, Reflections*. He read on and finally decided that "This weighty tome on dogmatics was nothing but fancy drivel" (Jung 1961, 57, 59).

His mother suggested that he read Goethe's *Faust*, and he did. At first he was deeply impressed. Goethe seemed to be a prophet. However, he could not forgive him for "having dismissed Mephistopheles by a mere trick, by a bit of jiggery-pokery" (Jung 1961, 60). Goethe had been a philosopher at one time, and obviously had learned something from philosophy before turning away from it. Jung turned to it, but all he found in his father's little library was Krug's *General Dictionary of the Philosophical Sciences* (1832), which is actually a rather substantial work. Jung read the article on "God" and found that the existence of God could not be proved. "What is wrong with these 'philosophers'? I wondered. Evidently they know of God only by hearsay. . . . Why do these philosophers pretend that God is an idea . . . when it is pefectly plain that He exists, as plain as a brick that falls on your head?" (Jung 1961, 61f.)

For Jung, as a boy in early puberty, God was "one of the most certain and immediate of experiences" because he had experienced grace in a particular episode when he was thirteen. Because of that experience, God was not an intellectual hypothesis for him but living reality (Jung 1961, 62).

Like Bliss Carman, the boy Jung searched for God and found him not in theology or philosophy but in nature, first in the realm of plants: ". . . the woods were the place where I felt closest to its deepest meaning and to its awe-inspiring workings." He found it, too, in Gothic cathedrals. "But there the infinity of the cosmos, the chaos of meaning and meaninglessness, of impersonal purpose and mechanical law, were wrapped in stone. . . . What I dimly felt to be my kinship with stone was the divine nature in both, in the dead and the living matter" (Jung 1961, 68).

Between his sixteenth and nineteenth years, Jung read Pythagoras, Heraclitus, Empedocles, and Plato. He also read Meister Eckhart. "Only in Meister Eckhart did I feel the breath of life—not that I understood him" (Jung 1961, 68f.). The scholastic philosophers repelled him: ". . . the Aristotelian intellectualism of St. Thomas appeared to me more lifeless than a desert" (Jung 1961, 69). "I thought, 'They all want to force something to come out by tricks of logic, something they have not been granted and do not really know about'" (Jung 1961, 69). He read Arthur Schopenhauer's *World as Will* (1818) and *Will in Nature* (1836). He was attracted by the philosopher's pessimism and agreed with it, but disappointed by Schopenhauer's theory that "the intellect need only confront the blind Will with its image in order to cause it to reverse itself" (Jung 1961, 70). What was the intellect but a fragment of the human soul? He turned to Immanuel Kant's *The Critique of Pure Reason*. Kant's *Ding an Sich* was more illuminating than Schopenhauer's blind Will, but it was a philosophical concept. Jung, at seventeen, demanded empirical evidence.

Consequently, he turned to science, and especially biology. At seventeen and eighteen, Jung was torn between science and the humanities, deeply drawn to both. In the sciences he was fascinated with zoology, paleontology, and geology.

Biology was an obvious enthusiasm because of his childhood love of nature and his rambles through the countryside during summer days. As a boy, he spent hours in close observation of the plant and animal world. Through his strolls through the nearby Jura hills, he also became aware of geological formations. From earliest childhood, he had no doubts at all about biological evolution and embraced Darwinism.

In the humanities he was primarily interested in prehistoric, Egyptian, and Greco-Roman archaeology. He read Latin as easily as he did German and was highly proficient in Greek as well. He was deeply read in the Greco-Roman classics and German literature.

However, during the late nineteenth century, only those with independent means could devote themselves either to scientific or archaeological research. In Jacob Burckhardt and Johann Jacob Bachofen, Jung had local Basel examples of highly productive scholars such as he would liked to have become. They, however, were independently wealthy. As the son of a poor pastor, Jung's options were very limited. His parents worried about his future. How was he going to earn his living? As Jung's father ruefully told a friend, "The boy is interested in everything imaginable, but he does not know what he wants."

He would have liked to become an archaeologist, but the University of Basel had no department of archaeology, and his father did not have the funds to send him anywhere else. Zoology was another possibility, but the only viable career choice was gymnasium (high school) teaching, and that did not appeal to him at all. Medicine, however, was a possibility. Thanks to his father's contacts, he was given a scholarship that made it possible for him to enter medical school at the University of Basel in 1896. An uncle also provided a loan. Like Freud, he had no vocation to be a healer. However, it involved science and, for that reason, he opted to become a physician.

Jung continued to read Schopenhauer and Kant. He had become totally disaffected with organized religion and so, instead of going to church with the family on Sunday mornings, he devoted that time to his philosophical studies. When he was around nineteen, he read Eduard von Hartmann's *The Philosophy of the Unconscious* (1869). He also read Carl Gustav Carus (1789-1869), a physician and artist who wrote *Psyche*. The latter begins: "The key to the knowledge of the nature of the soul's conscious life lies in the realm of the unconscious." Henri Ellenberger (1970, 207) notes that "Carus defined psychology as 'the science of the soul's development from the unconscious to the conscious.'"

During the middle years of the nineteenth century, the concept of the unconscious was discussed by a school of thought that appeared in Germany known as *Naturphilosophie* (nature philosophy). It was founded by the philosopher Wilhelm von Schelling (1775-1854) and was an offshoot of romanticism. The school included both philosophers and scientists. According to Schelling, the phenomenal world of organic beings rose from the *Weltseele* (world soul) and can only be understood in terms of underlying spiritual realities, not mechanical and physical laws alone. Humanity is inextricably bound up with the natural cosmos as an organized whole. Indirectly, at least, Schelling may have influenced Jung. Schelling postulated a mystical concept of the unconscious: *All-Sinn* is the "inner" or "universal" sense by which we understand the universe through mystical ecstasy, poetic or artistic inspiration, "magnetic somnambulism," or through dreams.

Other nature philosophers included Gotthilf Heinrich von Schubert (1780–1860), who regarded dreams as a universal symbolic language, and Ignaz Paul Vital Troxler (1780–1866), who taught philosophy at Basel and spoke of the successive emergence of higher degrees of consciousness. Troxler's concept of mental development was somewhat like Jung's theory of individuation (Ellenberger 1970, 206f.).

Henri Ellenberger detects similarities between certain concepts held by Freud and Jung and those of the nature philosophers. Noll takes a stronger position and asserts that Jung's concept of collective unconscious originated with them, as well as with the movement Noll and Mosse call *Völkischness*. Neither Freud nor Jung, however, mention the nature philosophers and *Völkisch* writers, nor acknowledge indebtedness to them. Neither do they mention Adolf Bastian, a world-traveling ethnologist whose concept of *Elementargedanken* somewhat resembles Jung's theory of archetypes. To my knowledge, Jung never read him.

The concept of the unconscious also occurred in many nineteenth-century novels, such as those of Honoré de Balzac, Edgar Allan Poe, Robert Louis Stevenson, Feodor Dostoyevsky, and many others. Indeed, both Freud and Jung readily acknowledged this.

Jung traced the concept of impersonal psyche to classical philosophy and was particularly interested in Gnosticism for that reason. He regarded alchemy as the bridge across the medieval era from the late classical Neoplatonists and Gnostics to his own work.

Experientially, awareness of the unconscious can be traced back to shamanism and faith healing. Their more recent counterparts were the esoteric doctrines of Madame Blavatsky's Theosophy, Spiritualism or Spiritism, tarot card reading, modern astrology, and geomancy. Scientifically minded investigators, such as the members of the British Society for Psychical Research, referred to these phenomena as parapsychology, which also included telepathy, psychokinesis, and what is now called ESP or extrasensory perception.

Spiritualism began with the Fox sisters in the United States during the 1840s. One of the sisters later admitted that she caused the so-called spirit rappings by cracking her toes. That, however, did little to discourage the fad, which had become very popular on both sides of the Atlantic by the 1890s. Jung was also fascinated by the prophecies of the Seeress of Prevorst, and shared the popular interest in the esoteric and occult. As Mircea Eliade shows, this interest coincided with the decline in traditional piety during the late nineteenth century. In literary and occult circles, the idea of the unconscious mind was bound up with what is now called parapsychology, as well as Spiritism. Many people experimented with séances, at which they tried to contact dead relatives and friends who had "passed over." They did so through mediums, usually women who went into trance states. During these trances, their minds were taken over by "controls" from "the other side" who spoke through their voices, saw through their eyes, and heard through their ears.

Most scientifically minded and rationalist people of the late nineteenth century ridiculed Spiritism, although there were conspicuous exceptions such as William James, the American philosopher and psychologist. They, however, became interested in the unconscious mind because of hypnotism. This technique, which began with Anton Mesmer during the late eighteenth century, was at first dismissed as bizarre and theatrical. However, some psychiatrists, such as Jean-Martin Charcot and Hippolyte Bernheim, experimented with hypnosis and found it to be a useful therapeutic procedure, especially with patients suffering from hysteria. It was through Charcot that Freud became aware of the unconscious (Ellenberger 1970, 89–101).

Jung discovered the unconscious mind through participating in family Spiritualist (or Spiritist) séances. He discovered Spiritualism in a thin volume on the subject by a clergyman when he was visiting a friend's house. The book was in the young man's father's library. Jung borrowed and read it. It whetted his appetite, and he read Sir William Crookes, Johann Karl Zöllner, and everything else he could find on the subject of Spiritualism. His own mother and several aunts were interested in séances because of Hélène (Helly) Preiswerk, a fifteen-year-old cousin of Jung's, who seemed to have mediumistic gifts. The women were holding séances at Jung's home. They sat around a table, hands touching, while Helly went into a trance. Soon she would announce that deceased family members such as his grandfathers were present, and she would pass on homely advice from them. Jung joined the séances and became fascinated in the psychological effects that the trance states had on Helly. Jung participated in the séances for two-and-a-half years, until he caught Helly cheating. She had a crush on him and made up things to please him. Jung did not believe in spooks, but was fascinated by the girl's remarkable revelations during trance states. What intrigued Jung was that, although Helly was poorly educated and not very bright, she expressed some very complex and abstruse philosophical ideas when she was in a trance, and also drew an intricate circular design to illustrate a complicated metaphysical philosophy. She was capable of none of this in a waking state. Also, in trance, Helly produced several distinct personalities, which Jung found that he could call up by hypnotic suggestion (Wehr 1988, 70).

"Of course I became deeply interested in all these things and began to try to explain them, something I could not do as I was only twenty-one at the time, and quite ignorant along these lines," he told a seminar audience in 1925 (Jung 1925, 4). Jung talked about séances and mediums to some of his fellow medical students, who scoffed at the occult but at the same time seemed uneasy whenever he discussed it with them.

Like all universities in the German-speaking world, Basel had a *Burschenschaft* or student fraternity, in this case a branch of Zofingia, a Swiss student association founded early in the nineteenth century. While most of the activities were social, members also held forums at which students presented papers for discussion. Some of these were later published in the fraternity journal. During his university years, Jung gave five talks, all of which were published. They have been assembled, translated, and published in 1983 by the Swiss analyst Marie-Louise von Franz in supplementary volume A of the *Collected Works of C. G. Jung* under the title *The Zofingia Lectures* (Jung 1896–99). This publication is a highly important contribution to our understanding of Jung because they are the earliest of his writings we have. They document the genesis of his concept of the unconscious.

The first of Jung's Zofingia lectures was "The Border Zones of Exact Science," which Jung presented in November 1896. It was a plea for open-mindedness and an invitation to explore parapsychological phenomena from the scientific perspective. In this and subsequent lectures, Jung also attacked positivism. Even as a young man in his late teens and early twenties, Jung insisted that nothing should be dismissed without first investigating it very thoroughly. To him, open-minded consideration of all new ideas and events was essential to science. For that reason, he was prepared to explore the evidence presented by Spiritualists and occultists.

In 1925, Jung told the seminar audience: "After this period, which contains the origin of all my ideas, I found Nietzsche." Jung was twenty-four when he read *Also Sprach Zarathustra*.

> I could not understand it, but it made a profound impression upon me, and I felt an analogy between it and the girl [Helly] in some peculiar way. Later, of course, I found that *Zarathustra* was written from the unconscious and is a picture of what that (sic) man should be. (Jung 1925, 6f.)

Jung finished his medical studies in 1900. After reading the preface to Richard von Krafft-Ebing's *Lehrbuch von Psychiatrie auf Klinische Grundlage*, 4th ed., (1890), he suddenly abandoned his plans to specialize in internal medicine and instead decided to become a psychiatrist, which was then a rather disreputable field. He accepted a post as a staff psychiatrist at Burghölzli Mental Hospital, which was connected with the University of Zürich. In 1900, he read Sigmund Freud's *Traumdeutung* (*The Interpretation of Dreams*), but did not understand it. "Then I returned to it in 1903 and found in it the connection with my own theories" (Jung 1925, 8).

Burghölzli's director, Eugen Bleuler, instructed Jung and his colleagues to pay close attention to the delusions, hallucinations, and babbling of psychotic patients. Bleuler was convinced that hidden meaning underlay these auditory and visual experiences. Jung was also directed to experiment with word association tests, in which hesitations in response to words repeated in series indicated blockages (Wehr 1988, 83–5). These clinical experiences gave Jung further empirical proof of the reality of the unconscious.

In 1906, Jung began a correspondence with Sigmund Freud, whom he visited in Vienna in 1907. A close friendship developed, as well as a collaboration. Jung became a psychoanalyst and Freud's "crown prince." However, although Jung was discreet about his dissent, he never fully subscribed to Freud's theory of the personal unconscious formed by chiefly sexual repression.

In late August of 1909, Freud, Jung, and a young psychoanalyst, Sandor Ferenczi, went to the United States, where Freud and Jung gave lectures at Clark University in Worcester, Massachusetts. Both had been invited by G. Stanley Hall, a prominent American psychologist and president of the university.

During the course of the New York-bound voyage aboard the North German Lloyd liner *George Washington*, Freud, Jung, and Ferenczi engaged in mutual dream analysis. In the course of analyzing one of Freud's dreams, Jung asked for more information and was briskly rebuffed. "But I cannot risk my authority!" Freud snapped. "At that moment he lost it altogether," Jung wrote years later. "That sentence burned itself into my memory; and in it the end of our relationship was already foreshadowed. Freud was placing personal authority above truth" (Jung 1961, 158).

During the crossing, Jung had a remarkable dream in which he found himself in a two-story house which was his, but which he did not know. As he made his way from the top floor to the basement, he found himself in rooms decorated in period designs. The top floor was rococo, the ground floor medieval; the basement had Roman walls. In a subbasement, he found moldering skulls and prehistoric potsherds. Freud interpreted the dream in terms of hidden death wishes, but Jung saw it as an invitation to explore deeper recesses of the psyche, and also as a revelation of impersonal depths of the unconscious (Jung 1961, 158f.).

In *Memories, Dreams, Reflections*, Jung claims that his first inkling of the collective unconscious was in the shipboard dream of the house followed by his mythic studies, beginning with Friedrich Creuzer's *Symbolik und Mythologie der alten Völker besonders der Griechen* (1810–1812). Creuzer was a Heidelberg classics professor who was a pioneer in mythic studies. According to Noll, Creuzer had profound impact on German scholars interested in Hellenistic mythology and the mystery cults. (I have read some of Creuzer myself, and find it incredibly dull.) Creuzer held that priests and hierophants transmitted an elite, esoteric doctrine, possibly derived from the "hidden wisdom" of India, Egypt, or the Old Testament, or even of prehistoric origin (Noll 1994, 179–181).

According to Richard Noll in *The Jung Cult*, Goethe, Wagner, and the German occultists were steeped in Creuzer because he stressed the impact of the irrational in the Hellenistic mystery religions. Indeed, Noll thinks that "Creuzer's work is the headwaters of the long, flowing intellectual current that extends from Goethe to Wagner to Jung" (Noll 1994, 180f.).

According to Noll, Jung assigned Creuzer to his three former Burghölzli assistants, Sabina Spielrein, Jan Nelken, and Johann Jacob Honegger. He also assigned them other books on archaeology and mythology, and had them collect clinical data from institutionalized patients that indicated evidence of "the phylogenetic layer of the unconscious mind" (Noll 1994, 181). If so, *Wandlungen und Symbole der Libido* was a collective enterprise. Noll attributes the origin of Jung's concept of the collective unconscious to his study of Creuzer. Perhaps, but I am far from being convinced.

In *Memories, Dreams, Reflections*, Jung wrote that his mythic studies ended in confusion until he found a key in an article by an old mentor, Henri Flournoy of Geneva. It was the case history of Miss Frank Miller, a young American woman in the prodromal stage of schizophrenia, who produced a series of poems that fascinated Jung because of their mythic motifs. They were to become the basis of *Wandlungen und Symbole der Libido*, which Peter Homans describes as an almost incomprehensible "shaggy dog story" and Noll as a *Völkisch* evocation of the solar cult that plays such an important role in Max Müller's theory of the origin of religion. Both Homans and Noll agree that *Wandlungen* is primarily a disclosure of Jung's inner meandering, that it is highly subjective, and that it best expresses his drive to free himself from Freud. I agree with the "shaggy dog story" criticism. The book is full of loose associations and also is badly written. I have some reservations with Noll's reduction of everything Jung thought and wrote to *Völkischness*, and do not agree that Max Müller's theories of the origin of religion were examples of that line of thought. *Wandlungen* is a complicated book, and I do not wish to linger on it here, but it must be mentioned in passing because it remains a controversial one. Was it Jung's declaration of independence from Freud, as Homans suggests? Was it Jung's delving into the solar cult, as Noll insists? Or, was it Jung's muddled attempt to work out his ideas about the collective unconscious?

My own often-repeated attempts to understand *Wandlungen* suggest to me Jung's confused grappling with ideas that he had not sorted out. In particular, he was fascinated with the impersonal dimensions of psyche, which he apprehended in a very uncertain and muddled way at that time, as well as with certain mythic themes that were then very widely discussed. These were the myths of the hero, which Lord Raglan, Otto Rank, and others pondered at length, and of the mother, which topic Johann Jacob Bachofen had opened for discussion. Nowhere in the original *Wandlungen* of 1912 does Jung discuss archetypes or the collective unconscious. For that reason, the English-speaking reader is not advised to base any conclusions about Jung's mind in 1912 on the 1954 translation of a rewrite by Jung, *Symbols of Transformation* (volume 5 of the *Collected Works*). M. Hinkle's 1916 translation, *The Psychology of the Unconscious*, is the English version of *Wandlungen und Symbole der Libido* as Jung published it in 1912.

In his famous BBC interview with John Freeman in 1959, Jung said that he discovered the collective unconscious when he reflected on an incident in which a patient at Burghölzli called him to the window, pointed to the sun and told him that there was a tube (or penis) hanging down from the sun, that it moved to the right and to the left, and that this was the origin of the wind. Jung said that he thought little about what the man had said until he chanced to read Albrecht Dieterich's little volume on a Mithraic text that had precisely the same motif. The fact that the patient had this mythic theme in mind suggested to Jung that all such motifs originate in an impersonal dimension of the unconscious shared with all human beings. Since the man had little education and had been in hospital for many years, it was highly unlikely that he had read Dieterich's book.

Noll has proven that the Solar Phallus Man was the patient of Johann Jacob Honegger, a young psychiatrist at Burghölzli who was one of Jung's assistants during the winter of 1909. According to Noll, Jung did not take credit for the patient until 1931 (Noll 1994, 182f.). In my reading of Jung's early essays, I have noted this discrepancy and wondered about it myself. Jung often repeated the story in later years, saying that the patient was his, and that this was how he discovered the collective unconscious. Indeed, Noll argues that Jung based his whole theory on this one incident. I do not agree with that, but it is true that Jung often told the story, and except for the one admission in an early essay, always said that the man had been his patient. How did Jung discover the collective unconscious? Since there is no mention of the concept in early papers such as "New Paths in Psychology" (1912), he does not appear to have worked out the concept of the collective unconscious at the time of his break with Freud. However, if his story of the dream of the house can be believed, he probably was groping with the idea of an impersonal dimension of the psyche during the late summer and autumn of 1909. He does not present it in *Wandlungen und Symbole der Libido* (1912), but it occurs in the later, revised editions including *Transformations of*

Symbols (volume 5 of *Collected Works*) which, as mentioned, is a completely rewritten version that Jung published in 1954.

Jung's most creative period was during the years between 1912 and 1918, a prolonged period of self-analysis. From comments by Barbara Hannah, Jung worked out his theories in collaboration with Antonia (Toni) Wolff, who had become his patient in 1911. Wolff was associated with the Jungs for forty years. She became Jung's confidant, possibly (though not certainly) his mistress, and played an important role in his work. Perhaps she was to Jung what Wilhelm Fliess was to Freud during 1896-1900, when he was engaged in the self-analysis that culminated in *The Interpretation of Dreams*.

One important facet of Jung's research was the recovery and analysis of early childhood fantasies and dreams. According to *Memories, Dreams, Reflections*, he made a return trip to the village of Klein-Hüningen near Basel, where he had spent most of his childhood and early youth. While he does not tell us when he made this trip, it was probably during the summer of 1913. Jung took up model town building with his son, a form of play which he had engaged in during his childhood, apparently, as he says in *Memories, Dreams, Reflections*, to aid in the recovery of early childhood memories.

According to *Memories, Dreams, Reflections*, beginning in December 1912 Jung had a series of hallucinatory visions that continued throughout World War I. According to the prefaces in volume 7 of *Collected Works* (*Two Essays on Analytical Psychology*), Jung first published his theory of the collective unconscious in 1916 in a brief paper in French entitled "La Structure de l'Inconscient" ("The Conception of the Unconscious"). Jung later expanded it into "The Relations Between the Ego and the Unconscious" (1916). Therefore, Jung worked out the concept of the collective unconscious during the four years between 1912 and 1916.

During this time, Jung made brief nocturnal notes of dreams in scribblers, one of which I have been shown I could read the German. It briefly described dream images in a sentence or two, giving the time when Jung had the dream. It is highly probable that Jung and Wolff were particularly interested in those dreams that seemed to have universal symbols or mythic motifs. However, no documentary evidence for that is as yet available. In 1916, as mentioned, Jung wrote and published his first papers on the subject of the collective unconscious. During 1918, when he was medical officer at a camp for British military detainees, Jung engaged in pointillist symbolic paintings in which he drew complex designs based on the mandalas that Hindu and Buddhist mystics sometimes use as meditation devices. By the end of World War I, Jung had worked out the basic premises of his own system, which he called analytical psychology.

I have the impression that this five- or six-year period of withdrawal was not an unhappy time of personal psychological crisis for Jung, but a time when he enjoyed a prolonged sabbatical in which he was engaged in research and writing. According to Peter Homans, it was the most creative period of his life, the time when he formulated his theories and principles. As with Freud, they were chiefly based on self-analysis or a form of introspection which, in those days, was a widely used technique of experimental psychology pioneered by Wilhelm Wundt. In the case of Freud and Jung, the technique was modified from perception to dream and fantasy analysis as the royal road to the unconscious.

By 1916, then, Jung had forged his own psychological system, analytical psychology. In that year, as mentioned, he published "The Structure of the Unconscious" in which he introduced the term *collective psyche*, which he subdivided into *collective mind* and *collective soul*. The first refers to "collective thinking" and the second to "the collective psychological functions as a whole." "Just as the individual is not merely a unique and separate being, but is also a social being, so the human mind is not a self-contained and wholly individual phenomenon, but also a collective one." Such a dual capability of the human mind exists because each of us is born with a brain that is highly differentiated: thus there is "a wide range of mental functioning which is neither developed ontogenetically nor acquired." There are facets in our mentality which are impersonal, collective, and universal. Because this is so, there is a remarkable correspondence in mythic motifs among widely separated peoples (Jung 1916, par. 454).

In 1917, Jung expanded on the collective unconscious in "On the Psychology of the Unconscious," which he subsequently revised four times. Here he showed that the collective unconscious is detached from the personal unconscious. The former is made up of "the most ancient and the most universal 'thought forms' of humanity," as well as inherited feelings. The collective unconscious is a hidden treasure on which humanity has drawn since primordial times (Jung 1917, 104, 66). These essays are found in volume 7 of Jung's *Collected Works*.

Two years later, in 1919, Jung introduced the term *archetypes* in "Instinct and the Unconscious," a paper he gave in London. After identifying the collective unconscious as "qualities which are not individually acquired but inherited," and stating that they are instincts or impulses without conscious motivation, Jung said: "In this 'deeper' stratum we also find the *a priori*, inborn forms of 'intuition,' namely the *archetypes* of perception and apprehension, which are the necessary *a priori* determinants of all psychic processes" (Jung 1919, 133).

Contrary to popular opinion, Jung did not coin the word archetype, a point that he frequently acknowledged himself. Instead, he said that he took it from certain classical and early Jewish and Christian sources such as Philo Judaeus, the *Corpus Hermeticum*, Dionysius the Areopagite, and Irenaeus (Jung 1954a, 5, 4).

According to Noll, Jung adopted the term *archetype* from *Naturphilosophie* (nature philosophy). The latter refers to certain schools of pre-Darwinian philosophers and writers which flourished between 1790 and 1830, the Romantic Era. In the course of their biological speculations about origins, some nature philosophers such as Richard Owen (1804–92) used the term *archetype* which *Webster's New Collegiate Dictionary* defines as "the original pattern or model of which all things of the same type are representations or copies." That, however, is not what Jung claimed as a source, and I see no good reason to doubt him.

In 1954, Jung published "On the Nature of the Psyche," (volume 8 of the *Collected Works*), in which he adopted the term *psychoid* (soul-like). Jung, as he acknowledged, derived the idea from his old mentor Eugen Bleuler, the director of Burghölzli Mental Hospital. According to Bleuler:

The *Psychoide* is the sum of all the purposive, mnemonic, and life-preserving functions of the body and central nervous system, with the exception of those cortical functions which we have always been accustomed to regard as psychic. . . . [thus] The body-psyche of the individual and the phylo-psyche together form a unity. (Jung 1954b, par. 368)

From suggestions by the atomic physicist, W. Pauli, Jung theorized the unity of space-time, psyche, and physis, not as a philosophical idea but as a scientific hypothesis (Jung 1952, par. 960). Therefore, in his final conception, the archetypes of the collective unconscious are the psychic components of physical being.

The collective unconscious is made up of archetypes: inherited biological tendencies that may have their origin in the sympathetic nervous system. Though formal and without content themselves, the archetypes manifest themselves in dream images, fantasies, fairy tales, and mythic motifs.

Jung sharply distinguished between the archetypes of the collective unconscious and the personal unconscious, the contents of which are acquired in the course of a person's life. The distinctions between personal and collective unconscious are essential in *Memories, Dreams, Reflections.* While Jung was interested in both his personal and archetypal experiences of the unconscious, it is clear that he was primarily concerned with the latter as breakthroughs into consciousness of the impersonal dimension of psyche shared with all human beings.

Jung's theory of the collective unconscious cannot be ascribed to any one factor. This is my chief quarrel with Noll, who thinks it can. At the same time, I agree that certain trends in German intellectual history influenced Jung. It was, after all, his climate of opinion, and he was bound to be influenced by what most thoughtful German-speaking people were reading and discussing at the time. Noll, however, grossly underestimates Jung's inner development and his own unique contributions. While none of his ideas were completely original, this is true of everyone. Henri Ellenberger traces nearly all of Freud's ideas as well as Jung's to nineteenth-century precedents, something that can be done with the ideas of all creative thinkers of the early twentieth century. The creative element is virtually always a matter of mixture and emphasis, the way ideas that are anything but original are shaped and focussed. Therefore, while this concept or that in Jung's thought can be traced to romanticism, nature philosophy, fin de siècle speculations, and to whatever "*Völkischness*" is, none of it explains Jung away. After all, Jesus never said anything original either. Even "love thy neighbor as thyself" was a quotation from the Book of Deuteronomy.

Neoromanticism, *Völkischness*, and *Bodenbeschafftenheit*

During the years between 1880 and 1900, several intellectual and cultural currents predominated in the German-speaking world. These included neoromanticism, *Völkischness*, fin de siècle thought, and *Bodenbeschafftenheit*. They had their counterparts in other European countries. They have been exhaustively discussed by Henri Ellenberger in *The Discovery of the Unconscious* (1970), and explored in depth by Richard Noll in *The Jung Cult: Origins of a Charismatic Movement* (1994). Here I want only to identify them and also to take issue with Noll, who attributes Jung's concepts solely to *Völkischness*.

Neoromanticism, to begin with, was a more or less bohemian literary movement that was urbane and sophisticated. I do not believe that it had any effect on Jung at all, or that he was even aware of it in parochial Switzerland. The fin de siècle thinkers were obsessed with decadence, and I do not see much evidence in Jung's early thought which shows impact from that quarter either. *Völkischness* is another matter.

According to George Mosse, the term *Völk* has a more comprehensive meaning to Germans than *Leute* or "people." Ever since the rise of German romanticism during the late eighteenth century, *Völk* has signified the "union of a group of people with a transcendent 'essence.'" The "essence" might be called nature, cosmos, or mythos. It is a spiritual value bound up with creativity, depth of feeling, individuality, and a sense of identity with other members of the *Völk*. Mosse's interest has been primarily because of its role in National Socialist ideology. Both he and Noll, however, emphasize the comprehensiveness of the viewpoint, and that the National Socialist ideology was only one of its outcomes. Many *Völkisch* writers such as Stefan Georg were hounded into exile by the Nazis and, in any case, to be a *Völkisch* thinker certainly did not imply that one was necessarily a National Socialist or had the least sympathy with that movement. Indeed, Mosse and Noll describe Zionism as a *Völkisch* movement. *Völkischness* was a romantic doctrine of ethnicity based on the inheritance of national traits emergent from geographical and prehistoric origins. It was also antimodern. It chiefly appealed to reactionaries who were bewildered by industrialism and the sudden dislocation of peoples. *Völkisch* thinkers deplored the decline of handcraft industries, the blighting of the countryside, and the disappearance of folk traditions. Switzerland was affected, and so was Jung. However, I see little difference between this viewpoint and that of some people in the ecological movement today. It was also very much like Gandhi's ideal of a *Darshan* India in which everyone wove cloth. In Britain, it took the form of the Luddite movement and the sentiments of William Blake and other romantic poets in their loathing of the "dark Satanic mills."

With respect to *Völkischness* and *Bodenbeschafftenheit*, I agree with Noll that both were important in Jung's thought, but with reservations. The latter is a concept that Laurens Van der Post explores in some depth in *Jung and the Story of Our Times* (1978) without, however, using the term. According to Noll, *Bodenbeschafftenheit* refers to "landscape mysticism." According to *Cassell's New German Dictionary*, the term means "condition of the soil, nature or quality of the soil." According to Mosse and Noll, *Völkischness* was a quasi-scientific doctrine that arose in Germany during the late nineteenth century. It was not an organized school of thought but a certain attitude or tendency in thinking that emphasized the subtle influences of geography, climate, and historical heritage on the people of a particular country. Its roots were in German romanticism. Its latter-day manifestations were highly diverse and included the intellectual basis of National Socialism, anti-Semitism, the mystique of national literature and art, and also the analytical psychology of Jung. The concept enjoyed the endorsement of German natural scientists such as Ernst Haeckel and Bernard Von Cotta. The latter stressed the influence of geological structure on national character in *Blut und Boden* (1853).

According to Noll, Jung first mentioned his interest in *Bodenbeschafftenheit* (though not by that name) in a letter to Freud of April 6, 1910, in which he said that he was reading Maurice Low's *The American People: A Study in National Psychology* (1909). In 1912, when he was in Buffalo, New York, Jung watched workers come out of a factory and amused an Anerican friend by remarking, "I should never have thought there was such a high percentage of Indian blood." His friend laughed and told him that there was not a drop of Indian blood in any of them. Jung then said it must be that geography shaped their appearance. He then invoked Franz Boas's anthropometric work to back his argument that geography affects the anatomy of second-generation immigrants. Later, he argued that the Jews are ill-suited for Europe because they originated in a dry, arid land. In 1918 in "The Role of the Unconscious" (in volume 10 of the *Collected Works*), Jung expounded a theory that the "lower half of the Germanic soul" is chthonic. In 1927, in the chapter "Mind and Earth" for Count Hermann Keyserling's *Mensch und Erde*, he expounded the theory that the human personality is profoundly conditioned by geology and geography.

Far from being a specifically Germanic idea, what Mosse and Noll call *Völkischness* or *Bodenbeschafftenheit* was known elsewhere by terms such as *geographical determinism*, a very widespread theory of history during the early years of the twentieth century among British and American historians. It is still held by many historians of differing national origins today.

A well-known example of a geographical determinist is Arnold Toynbee, with his theory of challenge and response in his seven-volume *A Study of History*. Toynbee argued that the character of a civilization is profoundly affected by geography and climate. According to Toynbee, the Athenian achievement can be traced to the poor quality of Attic soil as compared to the rich environs of neighboring Boeotia, where life was too easy. At the same time, the salubrious Athenian climate was mild enough to create a good working atmosphere and neither too hot nor too cold. He blamed the cultural impoverishment of the Eskimos on the harshness of the polar climate, which demanded that all energy be concentrated on survival. According to Toynbee, there have been twenty-one civilizations, each founded by creative minorities in response to geographical and ecological challenges.

It is not at all remarkable that Jung was attracted to geographical determinism, or *Völkischness*, because most scholars on both sides of the Atlantic shared its presuppositions during the late nineteenth and early twentieth centuries. Like biological evolution, it was an idea in the current intellectual milieu.

Whether or not Jung read specific studies by scholars who espoused the ideas, he was bound to be aware of them because of presuppositions in general discussion, in books and articles on various topics, and in trends of thought in the culture, generally. As in clothes and interior decorating, there are always fashions in ideas.

To me the problem with *Völkischness* is not only defining what it was, but what it was not. I fault Noll for defining *Völkischness* so broadly as to make the term useless. It was an outgrowth of German nationalism, and had its counterparts in Pan-Slavism, Zionism, Gallicism, and, for that matter, the American Dream or Manifest Destiny, but it should be distinguished from Madame Blavatsky's Theosophy, Spiritualism, nature philosophy, Nietzsche's Dionysianism, nudism, hiking, the solar cult, and a host of other nineteenth-century trends, fashions, and ideas with which Noll seems to identify it. For that reason, I prefer the less detailed but more precise discussion of *Völkischness* offered by George Mosse. Having said that, however, I also hasten to add that I agree that some aspects of Jung's thought are best explained in terms of this viewpoint, which was by no means peculiar to the Germans.

One of the chief characteristics of *Völkischness* was hostility to industrial progress and urbanism. Klein-Hüningen lost much of its rural character while Jung was growing up and, although he does not mention that specifically, there can be little doubt but that he deplored the expansion of the chemical industry in Klein-Basel through which he walked each day to and from school.

Unlike Noll, however, I do not see *Völkischness* as the prime source of Jung's concept of the collective unconscious. It was, however, a probable source of his idea of the geology of the human personality or *Bodenbeschaffenheit*. There was much thinking along these lines during Jung's formative years, and he was unquestionably affected by it. For the most part, however, he appears to have thought that his own ideas were original, which in some respects, they were.

Noll introduces the topic of nature mysticism as the basis of the geology of the personality. As Van der Post confirms, Jung certainly had the essence of this viewpoint in mind whether or not he actually used the term *Bodenbeschaffenheit*.

According to Ellenberger, a marked change occurred in European intellectual orientation in Europe around 1885, especially in the German-speaking countries. Indeed, as most intellectual historians concede, Germany rose to first rank in scientific, philosophical, and ideological leadership after the founding of the German Empire in 1871. At that time, Germany superseded France as the first power in continental Europe, and the once-dreamy Germans became galvanized with new energy. The German reputation for efficiency dates from the last two decades of the nineteenth century, whose achievements stem from the industrial revolution and accompanying advances in technology. In turn, the rise of German science and technology was accompanied by the rise of positivism and materialism among many German intellectuals.

While the young Freud was attuned to the new physics and biology and also strongly committed to positivism, Jung was repelled by materialism. Instead, he embraced the contrary and opposing intellectual movements that Ellenberger calls neoromanticism, Mosse and Noll *Völkischness*, and which also include concepts such as neovitalism. The latter, in particular, appealed to Jung. He was, in my view, only indirectly and more or less subconsciously affected by the other movements. Linked to these trends were other interests such as Spiritualism, the occult, Theosophy, and what Noll calls fin de siècle. These, taken together, constituted an opposition coalition against positivism. From the Zofingia lectures, it is clear that Jung, as a medical student, was in the camp of the neovitalists, neo-Kantians, neoromantics, Spiritualists, occultists, those who espoused *Völkischness*, and whoever else could be classed in the antimaterialist coalition. However, the fact that some of Jung's ideas were anticipated by others, such as Adolf Bastian and F. von Schubert, is only to say that he was a man of his age.

To some extent the antimaterialism of the late nineteenth century was a return to romanticism, and was therefore called neoromanticism. It did not, however, displace materialism and naturalism, but paralleled them to the end of the century. Neoromanticism affected philosophy, literature, the arts, music, and the general way of life.

In a narrower sense, neoromanticism in particular was the orientation of German poets such as Stefan George, Gerhard Hauptmann, Hugo von Hofmannsthal, and Rainer Maria

Rilke. In a broader sense it included the Pre-Raphaelites in Britain, the symbolists in France, and the *Jugendstil* movement in Germany. It culminated in "decadence" and the fin de siècle spirit (Ellenberger 1970, 278–84).

Jung was not affected by all of the currents and trends. The fin de siècle and "decadence" movements, for example, to which Oscar Wilde and Oswald Spengler belonged, did not affect him quite the way that it did them. Jung hated industrialism, urbanism, and modern technology, but was enthusiastic about scientific research and optimistic about the future. He was not part of the effete, defeatist, pessimistic school of nihilists who were impressed by the decline and fall of practically everything.

According to Ellenberger, neoromanticism was less a return to romanticism than a caricature of it. Thanks to urbanism and industrialism, neoromanticism did not have the poignant feelings of closeness to nature. In this respect, Jung was much closer to the old romanticism of the early nineteenth century, which did. According to Ellenberger, "Neo-Romanticists vizualized [nature] stylized as through artists' eyes, and those of esthetes." This was definitely not Jung's orientation at any time. Instead, he was more like the original romantics, who viewed everything in terms of growth and evolution. The neoromantics were obsessed with decadence; Jung was not. They were fascinated with the decline and death of past civilizations; such fascination was not Jung's view. Unlike Jung, the neoromantics had little empathy with peasants and country people and none with folklore. Instead, they had a vague but sophisticated fascination with myth. So did Jung, of course, and, in this respect, he was affected by the movement. Jung was also affected by the neoromantic emphasis on individualism and on seeing the individual in the larger context of interpersonal relationships, friendship, love, and in small groups rather than the masses. Neoromantics worshipped the individual to the point of isolation, and this tied in with Jung's introversion. Narcissus was a general symbol of the time, and Jung leaned toward narcissism.

In one important respect, however, Jung was very much attuned to the neoromantic spirit. Like the old romantics, the neoromantics were preoccupied with the irrational and the occult, and they chose to explore the hidden depths of the human mind. They were fascinated with the unconscious. Eduard von Hartmann, for example, was of this orientation although he wrote earlier. Ellenberger quotes Jules Romains on the *symbolistes*, the neoromantics of France. The *symbolistes*, he said, retreated to their ivory towers to tell themselves stories. They were bookish and childish. Many were preoccupied with decadence, fascinated with the decline of Rome, France of the *ancien régime*, and with Byzantium.

Neoromanticism, fin de siècle attitudes and thought, and German *Völkischness* were interrelated but distinctive tendencies in the European intellectual life of the last two decades of the nineteenth century. All three owed something to the long peace that had prevailed since Waterloo, and to the security of the age, especially among the high bourgeoisie and aristocracy. Revolutionary movements such as social democracy were rather peripheral. Instead, the ruling classes were as confident and serene as the Forsytes of Galsworthy's saga.

In large measure, fin de siècle *Weltschmerz*, or "world weariness," was a coffeehouse pose. Among Jung's fellow Zofingians in the Breo, their favorite Basel beer hall, all of these topics and more were probably discussed. They included speculative chat about mediums and spiritualist séances, Theosophy, Nietzche, hypnosis, somnambulism, dual personality, and psychosis as mental degeneration. In many ways, neoromanticism was like the New Age today. Like the latter, it was apolitical, bohemian, aesthetic, and vaguely mystical. Like the New Age, neoromanticism was hostile to the traditional religious establishment and sympathetic to alternatives such as the revivals of Wotanism, occultism, and the Westernized forms of Hinduism, Buddhism, and Taoism which were introduced by traveling swamis, and European converts to Eastern religions.

The intellectual origins of Jung's concept of the impersonal psyche can be traced in part to certain trends in late nineteenth-century German intellectual history. In *Politics and the Sciences of Culture in Germany: 1840–1970* (1991), Woodruff D. Smith discusses *Völkerpsychologie*, a German cultural science that perished during the 1920s and that was unknown outside the German-speaking countries. It was a comparative study of the characteristic mental patterns of various ethnic groups with emphasis on their historical development. As such it was therefore quite close to what Noll calls *Bo-denbeschaffenheit*. It originated during the 1850s as one of the responses to the failure of liberalism in Germany, and, during the late nineteenth century, was connected with liberal anthropology. In Germany, *Völkerpsychologie* was an academic discipline. One of its founders, Theodore Waitz, was distressed by the unwillingness of the great mass of people to act rationally and to support liberalism and democracy. *Völkerpsychologie* therefore had a political agenda.

One of its founders and adherents was Adolf Bastian (1826–1905), a world-traveling ethnologist whose theories anticipated Jung's. As a result of his travels, Bastian was convinced of the psychic unity of humanity. He held that mental phenomena were the results of brain physiology, the impingement of the environment, and innate ideas. Brain anatomy and physiology are uniform throughout the world; so too is the basic structure of ideas. Bastian called this basic mental structure *Elementargedanken* or elementary ideas. The late Joseph Campbell often compared Bastian's "elementary ideas" to Jung's archetypes of the collective unconscious. However, there is no evidence that Jung was aware of Bastian's thought during his formative years. According to Bastian, cultural concepts and ideas are superimposed on "elementary ideas." He called them *Völkergedanken*. A major difference between Bastian and Jung is that the former's concepts were rather fuzzy and not based on scientific research (Ellenberger 1970, 730).

Wilhelm Wundt (1832–1920), whom some historians call the father of modern psychology, was also an adherent of *Völkerpsychologie*. According to him, the innate structure of the human mind largely shapes social development. He attempted to identify the mental disposition, or *Völkseele*, that characterized each stage of development. Every people has its own unique *Völkseele*, which differs from others at the same stage of development. Certain elements of culture are crucial, such as language, myth, and custom. According to Smith, Wundt's work was the last gasp of *Völkerpsychologie* (Smith 1991, 116–27).

Jung was affected by some aspects of the antimaterialist revolt and ignored others. What is more, while he reacted against the equally powerful positivist and materialist trends that inspired Freud, there also are identifiable aspects of positivism in Jung's viewpoint. These appear in his choice of science over the humanities and also in his rejection of orthodox Christianity.

Jung was apolitical, and so we must not expect him to espouse those aspects of *Völkischness* which were part of the Germanic political agenda, or even the Helvetic. His interests were biological, psychological, parapsychological, and religious. Many matters of great concern to other people of his time, such as politics, were peripheral to him and remained so. By 1900, when he finished medical school and left for Zürich, he had already formed the basic concepts that he was to espouse for the rest of his life. He was convinced of the reality of the unconscious mind. At that time, however, his ideas were fuzzy, muddled, and undeveloped. In turn, their origin lay in experiences and thoughts that were much earlier than his Spiritualist séances with Helly Preiswerk in 1896, and that are, indeed, traceable to his early childhood.

The ideas of Freud and Jung were resisted by psychologists and psychiatrists of the early twentieth century. Indeed, Jung cited the example of Galileo in his defense of Freud in the preface to *The Psychology of Dementia Praecox* (1907).

> My attention was drawn to Freud by the first book of his I happened to read, *The Interpretation of Dreams*, after which I also studied his other writings. I can assure you that in the beginning I naturally entertained all the objections that are customarily made against Freud in the literature. But, I told myself, Freud could be refuted only by one who has made repeated use of the psychoanalytic method and who really investigates as Freud does. . . . He who does not or cannot do this should not pronounce judgment on Freud, else he acts like those notorious men of science who disdained to look through Galileo's telescope. (Jung 1907, 3f.)

In his youth as a medical student, intern, and budding young scientist, Jung was exceptionally open to new ideas. In his teenage arguments with his father, his youthful Zofingia papers, as a medical student, and as an apologist for Sigmund Freud, Jung vigorously insisted that no idea should be rejected until it had been thoroughly investigated, and that there were many apparently bizarre topics such as parapsychology which deserved serious consideration. This attitude underlay Jung's sympathetic study of Spiritualism, psychokinetic phenomena, astrology, and alchemy. It was also the reason for his defense of Freud. In all of these areas, Jung lived up to his own principle by becoming very knowledgeable in fields despised or rejected without proper study by academics. In part, this enterprise reflected his own youthfulness and intellectual flexibility. Such open-mindedness was also a lifelong aspect of his character. The octogenarian Jung was very interested in UFOs, for example, and accumulated a large file of data on the subject. His interest in National Socialism was inspired by the same attitude.

To Paul Stern, Jung was a failed prophet. According to Richard Noll, he was a mystic who founded a charismatic cult. In my view neither is correct. Prophets receive divine revelations which they impart in pure form, and are therefore mediums of divine self-disclosure, usually through angelic visitations, visions, audible messages, or some other miraculous vehicle of supernatural will. At no time did Jung ever make such claims. Mystics usually achieve supernatural illumination through ascetic disciplines and meditation. Jung *could* be classed as a mystic. He did have visions and inner religious experiences that were much like those of the Friends, with their doctrine of Inner Light. He can also be compared with the practitioners of Zen, Hindu *rishis*, Islamic Sufis, and the Kabbalists among Jewish mystics. But his mysticism was very private, and indeed secretive, and he always denied wanting to found a Jungian cult. His mysticism was of a very different character, moreover, from his psychological experiences, which were realizations of the archetypes of the collective unconscious. Instead, Jung, like all mystics, had conscious experiences of what he claimed to be the supernatural, which did not come from within himself but without.

To conclude, as a man of the late nineteenth and early twentieth centuries, Jung was affected by many of the intellectual and cultural movements of his day. He was drawn to some, such as esotericism and the occult, while he was repelled by positivism and all forms of dogmatism, Marxism, and communism.

Jung can be faulted for the inadequacy of his verification techniques and for refusing to submit his theories to the critical scrutiny of academe. By surrounding himself with admiring followers, he isolated himself and missed the benefits of critical dialogue. This latter, in my view, was his most grievous failing, and is the principal reason why his psychological theories are not highly regarded by psychologists other than those of the analyical school. In that respect, both psychoanalysis and analytical psychology now have some of the characteristics of cults. Both have authoritative texts, special seminaries for the training of practitioners, their own journals and conferences, and, above all, a body of doctrine. Jungianism and Freudianism are now cults in the sense of being closed systems, though Jung in particular would not have approved of this development.

Two

Explorer of the Human Soul

Kesswil and Lake Constance

According to the civic records of Basel Stadt, Carl Gustav Jung was born at 7:32 P.M. on July 26, 1875, in the Swiss Reformed Church parsonage at Kesswil in the Canton of Thurgau (sometimes spelled Thurgovia). A plaque in the parsonage wall at Kesswil appropriately commemorates him: IN THIS HOUSE WAS BORN CARL GUSTAV JUNG, JULY 26, 1875–1961, EXPLORER OF THE HUMAN SOUL AND ITS HIDDEN DEPTHS.

C. G. Jung was the second child of the Reverend Dr. Johann Paul Jung (1842–1896), a Swiss Reformed Church pastor, and Emilie née Preiswerk (1848–1923). The firstborn son, Paul, had died a few days after his birth two years before. In 1884, when Carl was nine, his sister Johanna Gertrude (Trudi) was born. She died in 1935 (Wehr 1988, 9).

Jung's father was the thirteenth son of Carl Gustav Jung (1794–1864), a German physician from Mannheim whose forebears lived in the Rhineland city of Mainz. In later years, Jung traced his paternal ancestry back to the late seventeenth century. Because the French burned the *Rathaus* and its records, he could not trace them earlier than 1683. However, he did learn that there had been a Dr. Carl Jung in Mainz during the early seventeenth century and, in all probability, the family of physicians had been in Mainz since medieval times. Their ethnic ancestors were Franks.

According to family mythology, Jung's paternal grandfather was the illegitimate son of Goethe, a connection which his grandson constantly denied but, at the same time, often mentioned. Exiled from his beloved Germany because of the oppressive Metternich regime, the first Carl Gustav went to Paris where he was befriended by the geographer Alexander Humboldt who recommended him for a university teaching post in Basel. Jung often said that he was only half Swiss because of his grandfather's origins. Carl Gustav I soon made a name for himself as a reformer of the decrepit medical academy at the University of Basel, and also as a physician. Indeed, the anatomist Wilhelm His of Leipzig said of him: "In Jung, Basel possessed an unusually full and rich human nature. Thanks to his spirit, Jung gladdened and refreshed his fellow men for many decades; his creative strength and his warm devotion bore fruit . . . that benefited the sick and needy above all" (Wehr 1988, 15f.). Jung the elder became the rector of the university, the European equivalent of university president. Among other achievements, the elder Jung enlarged the citizens' hospital and also founded The Institute of Hope, a home for feeble-minded children.

Johann Paul, Jung's father, was the thirteenth son. His mother, Sophie Frey, was Carl Gustav Jung the elder's third wife. Family fortunes were in decline. Nevertheless, Johann Paul went to Göttingen University where he studied Semitic languages, especially Hebrew and Arabic. He finished his studies and earned a doctorate. However, the Jungs suffered financial reverses and his father lacked funds for the son's official qualification in philology, necessary for an academic post. At that critical moment, a relative died leaving a sum of money for the education of a family member "who had the desire to become a minister" (Wehr 1988, 20). It solved Paul's problem financially, but at considerable cost to him personally. Out of expediency, it seems, he became a minister without religious vocation although he would rather have had an academic career. He became an impoverished Reformed Church pastor, with little financial inheritance, who served country parishes in the Swiss Rhineland.

In 1873, he married Emilie, the thirteenth child of the Reverend Samuel Preiswerk (1799–1871), who was the head vicar or Antistes of Basel. Preiswerk was of a distinguished clerical family. C. G. Jung had six uncles on his mother's side who were Swiss Reformed pastors. Samuel Preiswerk was a Hebrew scholar who wrote a Hebrew grammar and edited a monthly journal, *Morgenland*, which advocated the Jewish settlement of Palestine long before Theodore Herzl founded the Zionist movement in Basel in 1897. According to Jung, "He was not only highly learned, but also had a pronounced poetical mind; indeed, he had a rather peculiar mind." Preiswerk thought that he was constantly surrounded by spirits and that his daughter Emilie had to stand behind him because a living person behind him would scare them off. Indeed, Samuel Preiswerk was very interested in the occult as well as in Spiritualism. Albert Oeri calls him "a visionary who experienced whole dramatic scenes, complete with conversations with spirits" (Wehr 1988, 17).

The Preiswerk family was more than a little odd, and his mother Emilie, who was also rather peculiar, might have passed it on to Jung himself. Jung's maternal grandmother was comatose for thirty-six hours during a youthful bout with scarlet fever. For that reason, according to some, she had "second sight" (Wehr 1988, 17f.).

In *Memories, Dreams, Reflections*, Jung is far more impressed by his mother than by his father who, in my view, he underestimated. His most vivid recollections of his mother concerned what he called her "Personality Number Two," his rather prosaic term for an uncanny, frightening unconscious personality that occasionally emerged, usually unexpectedly. "She would then speak as if talking to herself, but what she said was aimed at me and usually struck to the core of my being, so that I was stunned into silence" (Jung 1961, 48f.).

Jung attributed great significance to ethnicity. In his own case, his mother's family, the Preiswerks, had been in Basel for around five hundred years. Like most German-speaking Swiss, they were of Alemannic descent. The Alemans were a Teutonic nation that joined the Swabian Confederation during the fourth century C.E. Their ancestors, like all Germans, originated in the heaths of Baltic Germany, Denmark, and Sweden around 2000 B.C.E. Jung was fascinated by reports of mummified neolithic bodies found in peat bogs, which he read about shortly before taking ship for America during the late summer of 1909. In *Memories, Dreams. Reflections*, Jung makes many references to his mother's Alemannic ancestors, especially in the dream just before her death, when he found himself in a wild landscape and trembled at the approach of Wotan, the

Wild Huntsman, who came with his hounds to gather a soul to the *sälig lut*, or "Blessed Folk" (Jung 1961, 313f.). He attributed the strangeness of his mother's nighttime personality to her ancient forebears. He made much less of his father's Frankish ancestry.

To Jung, family inheritance was an important determinant, and he attributed much in his own psychic make up to the Preiswerks. As mentioned, his grandfather Samuel was a strange man who dabbled in the occult. He, his daughter Emilie, and Carl Jung himself all had the alter ego which Jung referred to as Personality Number Two. Materially speaking, Samuel was in dire financial straits during his last years and Emilie inherited very little. The Jungs were always the poor relations of the Preiswerks and frequently dependent on family charity, which was grudgingly given. Carl Jung did not like the Preiswerks, who were highly intrusive, and may have moved from Basel to escape them. Even in his later years, he wrote correspondents that he had no desire to go to Basel, even for a visit.

After their marriage in 1873, Jung's parents were sent to Kesswil, it being the usual practice then and now for young, recently ordained ministers to be called to small rural parishes for their apprenticeship years. It is not usually a matter of choice or preference on the minister's part. Paul Jung was highly conscientious and devoted himself completely to his ministry. However, as his son wrote, his heart was not in it, and he often mooned dreamily about his student days, smoked a long student pipe, and sang student songs like *"Alle schweige, alle neige."* I think that he was a misfit in the ministry. There was little that he could do to keep up his academic interests in the little Rhenish villages where he spent his life, trying to do something for which he was emotionally unsuited.

In *Memories, Dreams, Reflections*, Jung does no more than mention Kesswil as his birthplace. In terms of astrology, *Bodenbeschaffenheit*, and *Völkischness*, however, the time and place of every person's birth are important determinants. According to Laurens Van der Post, one of Jung's friends of his late years, Jung strongly held this viewpoint and therefore considered his own birthplace and time of birth significant determinants of his destiny. It is also possible that he considered the birthplace important in terms of subtle forces of some kind upon the unconscious of a very young infant. In *Jung and the Story of Our Times*, Laurens Van der Post emphasized Jung's origins, and mentioned conversations in which Jung spoke of his birthplace near Lake Constance and the proximity of the Rhine during his boyhood as important psychophysical determinants (Van der Post 1978, 64f.).

In 1909, Jung became interested in astrology, and, in later years, often cast horoscopes for his patients, which he used in diagnosis. He was impressed with their accuracy in many cases and concluded that the archaic astrologers had stumbled onto natural laws which had nothing to do with astronomical phenomena but which evoked the archetypes of the collective unconscious. Later, during the 1920s, Richard Wilhelm, an associate of Count Keyserling, an occultist, introduced Jung to the I Ching and also to Chinese geomancy. While Jung makes no mention of *feng shui*, (Wind and Water), the Chinese geomantic practice, it is apparent that he was fascinated with traditional Chinese lore concerning the subtle impact of natural geographical and meteorological forces on the psyche. In retrospect, he interpreted his own time and place of birth in these terms. Thus, Jung took both astrology and *Völkischness* seriously, the former as an archaic form of depth psychology, and the second as a mystical determinant emergent from the landscape, what Richard Noll calls *Bodenbeschafftenheit*.

When Carl was six months old, the family moved to Laufen near the Falls of the Rhine. He therefore had no conscious recollection of the place of his birth until his mother took him to Lake Constance when he was three. He did, however, imply to Van der Post that Kesswil and Lake Constance had unconscious impact on him.

Kesswil is a tiny village not far from the reedy south shore of Lake Constance, which Germans call Bodensee. It is near Romanshorn, presumably the port where he and his mother took the lake steamer to an island where his mother had friends who lived in a castle. The island may have been Mainau. His early memories of Lake Constance are only of this excursion and the deep impression which the lake made on him.

Lake Constance (*Boden See*) is a brooding body of water. It is the largest lake in the German-speaking world: Austria, Germany, and Switzerland border it. Being shallow, the lake is sometimes stormy and turbulent. Usually, however, it is calm, under hazy skies. It is vast; an inland sea. Indeed, if one stands on the Swiss shore near Kesswil one cannot see across it. The effect is that of being on the edge of a vast ocean. It is a basin of the Rhine, which rises in the glacial lakes of Alpine Grisons in eastern Switzerland and flows into the lake at its eastern end. The Rhine flows out again at the German city of Constance in the west, through the Rhineland, which is the borderland between Germanic and Latin Europe. Finally, having traveled nearly a thousand miles, the Rhine expires in the five arms of the Dutch Delta on the North Sea.

According to Van der Post, Jung held that "nature in all its forms was not a cold, impersonal, objective reality but was rather an expression of symbolic form, evocative of all that was symbolic within the spirit of man." Van der Post thought that Jung believed that the water of lake and river was a basic element in the "opening movement of the orchestration of his own spirit." Based on the I Ching, to which Jung was introduced by Richard Wilhelm, the water of the lake reflects the sky and thus unites the dark, earthy *yin* principle and the light, celestial *yang*, the two opposites of reality. The I Ching personifies the lake as a feminine promise of future increase. According to Van der Post, "A lake is a macrocosmic sea microcosmically contained in the earth . . . a comprehensible source of nourishment to the life and spirit of man." The river is water in motion finding its way through ravines, cataracts, and gorges to the sea. "The Rhine," Van der Post wrote, "is one of the great mythological rivers of the world . . . a dark, angry, and outraged masculine stream. It is as dark and in as strange a rage and passion to reach the sea as is the Congo issuing straight out of the darkest centre of the heart of darkness of my native Africa" (Van der Post 1978, 66f.).

The Swiss countryside on the south shore of Lake Constance is a checkerboard of wheat fields and orchards, what the travel writer Murray called "the garden and granary of Helvetia." Jung was a Swiss of the Central European Alpine land, which Jung compared to a mussel shell. "The people who sit in the shell and round its rim are the Swiss, and that's me" (Jung 1906–1961, 2:419).

According to Jung, astrologically speaking, the Swiss astrological sign is either the feminine, earthly Virgo or the masculine, creative sign Taurus. As Jung put it, "This old psychological understanding expresses the fact that what is contained within the mother is a creative seed that will one day burst forth." He saw the union of the masculine and feminine in the two zodiacal signs. To that he attributed Swiss unapproachability and stubbornness, and also the "'*principium individuationis*' as a supreme union of opposites." Because he was Swiss, these traits also applied to himself (Wehr 1988, 12).

According to Jung, astrology is an archaic form of psychodynamic psychology, and the archetypes of the collective unconscious are evoked in such unlikely ways as the alleged influences of particular planetary combinations at the moment of conception or birth. He also attributed unconscious formative influences on the newborn of the subtle impact of wind, water, terrain, and other geographical features of the birthplace. Jung took both astrology and *Bodenbeschafftenheit* seriously as psychological determinants. According to Greta Jung-Baumann, his daughter, Jung was impelled to become an explorer of the hidden depths of the soul by his birth sign, Leo, and the planetary positions at 7:32 A.M., 1875, the moment of his birth (Baumann-Jung 1975, 35). Marie-Louise von Franz attributes significance to Jung having been born when Nietzsche was proclaiming "the death of God." That she thought so typifies fin de siècle pessimism, which she may have imbibed from Jung. Historically, the year 1875, that of Jung's birth, marks the dawn of what Carleton Hayes calls "The Age of Materialism." It is certainly true that positivism was gaining momentum in the Germanies during the 1870s because of the industrial revolution. These were Jung's early orientations in time and space.

According to Jung, Van der Post, and von Franz, the scene of one's birth and early years, the time, and the historical context affect the psyche as unconscious, archetypal forces that give rise to dream images, fantasies, and visions even in the mind of a young child. In Jung's view, the consciousness of a young child is very fragile, and fragmented like an archipelago of islands. Nearly all of the psyche of a very young infant is made up of the archetypal or collective unconscious, just as it is in animals. It is instinctual. Ego develops later. Therefore, the memories of early dreams, fantasies, and visions are of archetypal experiences.

In terms of *Bodenbeschafftenheit*, the scenes of Jung's infancy combined the proximity of both deep and rushing water with the distant prospect of the Alps to the south and the gentle, rolling countryside between them. Of these geographical features, water was the most important. According to Van der Post, Jung often said that everyone needs the presence of water, and that it was important to him to have been born near the shores of a lake and to have grown up near the banks of a river.

Jung's *Völkischness* appears in his remark to Van der Post that German national character developed as it did because of the dark German soil. Jung told him that any race that settled in Germany would, in time, acquire some of the fundamental aspects of what we now identify as German character. He thought the same of his own country, and said that if Tartars had settled in Switzerland, they would, in time, have become stolid like the Swiss. (Indeed, Huns did settle in certain remote Alpine districts of Switzerland after the defeat of Attila, but there is no evidence that they ceased to be like their Mongolian ancestors. Indeed, they continued to practice shamanism and to preserve their ethnic identity in isolation until the little community finally died out during the fifth century C.E.)

Jung never abandoned his *Bodenbeschafftenheit*, and, as mentioned, when he was in Buffalo, New York, he thought that the workmen emerging from a plant looked like Indians. It was part of his *Bodenbeschafftenheit* to regard water in the same way. Still waters evoke the collective unconscious while the rushing waters of a river call up archetypes more dynamic. Jung was fascinated with references to rivers, streams, lakes, and the sea in fairy tales, myths, and esoteric writings. He regarded them as archetypal images. He held that people all over the world have experienced the water symbol in dreams and myths since primordial times, and that such images are rooted in our prehistoric ancestry.

The aforementioned visit to Lake Constance when he was three made a profound impression on the boy. Of it, Jung writes:

> The waves of the steamer washed up to the shore, the sun glistened on the water, and the sand under the water had been curled into little ridges by the waves. The lake stretched away

and away into the distance. This expanse of water was an inconceivable pleasure to me, an incomparable splendor. At that time the idea became fixed in my mind that I must live near a lake; without water, I thought, nobody could live at all. (Jung 1961, 7)

In his later years, Jung received many letters from correspondents who had experienced watery depths in the way he did. A clergyman wrote him of a dream he had had of a dark and uncanny lake. He was seized with panic and woke (Jung 1954a, par. 40). To Jung this was a typical example of an archetypal dream, the watery depths being a symbol of the collective unconscious.

The dream was a *descensus ad inferos*, or downward journey into the underworld or depths of the sea in mythology that symbolized a psychic realization of inner depths. Jung wrote: "We must surely go the way of the waters, which always tend downward, if we would raise up the treasure . . ." (Jung 1954a, par. 37).

In Jung's view, myths are the symbolic expressions of the archetypes of the collective unconscious. Thus, the origin of the hero's plunge into the depths to find the plant that gives eternal life in *The Epic of Gilgamesh* is a symbol of the water archetype. The same is also true of the Siberian and North American cosmological myths of the diving animal. In these stories, a creator animal such as a beaver or otter dives to the bottom of a lake and brings up the mud from which either the animal or a creator god makes the world. Jung often spoke of the mythic image that he called "the treasure hard to find," in which the hero descends to the bottom of the sea to find a precious stone. This theme is closely related to that of the dragon, in which a monster who can make no use of the treasure nonetheless guards it from theft. Jung used the term *mythologem*, by which he meant a fragment of myth as a symbolic expression of an unconscious or archetypal impulse. Such themes, he said, continue to surface in the dreams and fantasies of modern people in terms of entirely modern imagery: UFOs, for example. Such images are drawn from an individual life experience or from the perceived world of sensation, but are basically from the collective unconscious.

The Falls of the Rhine

During the winter of 1875–6, the Reverend Johann Paul Achilles Jung was called to the Swiss Reformed parish of Laufen near the Rhine Falls. In Switzerland, the churches of all officially recognized denominations are tax-supported cantonal properties, and the clergy are cantonal officials whose duties include the conduct of funerals, the keeping of vital statistics, and other such matters. This system still prevails today. At the same time, since the Reverend Jung was a citizen of Basel, he was actually an alien both in Thurgau and Laufen. The latter is in the canton of Zürich. As such, his parochial tenure and transfers were the responsibility of the consistory of Basel, to which he belonged.

Even today, Laufen is a country parish on the right bank of the Rhine and very much as it was when Jung was taken there by his parents at the age of six months. It consists of a very imposing church, the huge three-story manse next to it, and, across the road, the quaint low brick house of the sexton. The present occupants of the latter keep a lovely flower garden. Part of the house appears to have been stables at one time; undoubtedly they were so during Jung's infancy. Behind the sexton's house, and to the left, stretches a meadow which figured in Jung's most vivid childhood dream. It is framed by a stand of trees, beyond which are farmer's fields. Also on the left, and just before one reaches the sexton's house, there is an old graveyard where the infant Jung witnessed burials. The laundry house mentioned in *Memories, Dreams, Reflections* is gone, but it would have been near the manse, near the south bank of the Rhine. A road curves right and past the manse and church to Laufen castle, which is now a restaurant. The restaurant and the nearby parking lot are new. Otherwise, Laufen is exactly as Jung describes it in *Memories, Dreams, Reflections*. Van der Post speaks of being overwhelmed by the vividness of the place, the impact of the dramatic falls, the floral beauty of the gardens, and the imposing church. My own impressions were quite different. I found it to be a quiet place; the falls are barely audible when one is at the manse, and the scene is bucolic.

What Jung calls the Dachsen Road is now a two-lane paved highway which leads south. I do not recall seeing the hill down which a robed priest strode who frightened him when he was three and a half, nor do I recall seeing the Alps in the distance. However, it was near nightfall when I visited Laufen. The whole area is thickly wooded and very beautiful.

Today, a well-kept path winds through the woods to the railroad bridge which now, as in Jung's infancy, crosses the Rhine just above the falls. There are walkways for pedestrians on either side, guard rails, and, if I recall correctly, a protective mesh that probably was not there in Jung's early childhood. Here, as he was later told, he once nearly slipped through the rails and was rescued just in time by the maid. I could see how easily it could have happened when there were only the guard rails and their stanchions. The roar of the falls immediately becomes very loud as one makes one's way down through the woods to the bridge. But, as mentioned, it is remarkably muted when one is at the church, the manse, or at Laufen Castle.

I made my visit by train from Zürich to Schaffhausen, which is a Swiss enclave on the north side of the Rhine surrounded on three sides by Germany. Schaffhausen is now a fairly large town dominated by the Castle of Mûnot on the hills that rise above the town. It is an easy walk from the railroad station to the Rhine above the falls. Road signs point west to Constance, where the reborn Rhine flows from the lake. I strolled beside the calmly flowing Rhine, and then down a city street to Neuhausen, now part of Schaffhausen but then a village, where signs pointed to a road that curves left and down a fairly steep incline. When he was an infant, the maid, whom Jung later regarded as his archetypal anima, used to take him to Neuhausen. Perhaps she also took him with her to Schaffhausen and to the Castle of Mûnot.

Some commentators are skeptical of Jung's childhood memories, arguing that an octogenarian would not recall such long-ago scenes and events. I disagree. I remember an incident in 1927 when I was three when I was taken by my father to a hangar on Bolling Field where we stood next to *The Spirit of St. Louis*. He took me there because I came down with the measles just when I was hoping to see Lucky Lindy, whom I thought was coming to Washington to see me. Even now, I can remember what I hoped for and thought when I was three, my keen disappointment at missing Lindy's visit to Washington, but also the awe I felt as my father and I stood together in the semidarkness of the hangar, just the two of us and *The Spirit of St. Louis.*

I also recall a dream I had when I was around three and a half in which my father and I walked up a hill near our house in Anacostia. In the dream, I looked back to see my mother, with a very sad look on her face, as she disintegrated like the bark of a tree. Aniela Jaffé, to whom I told the dream, told me that it was an archetypal dream and that it meant that my mother was immortal.

In my own case, I know that I recall such memories because I have renewed the memory traces many times during the course of my life. I rarely recover early memories which I have not retraced many times. Consequently, I regard my childhood memories as highly polluted, faint echoes of original memories that might be recovered in pure form under hypnosis but which are not consciously available to me otherwise. I rather think that this is true of most people, perhaps everyone. In other words, I do not think that we can get back to a pure early memory except perhaps under hypnosis. Even then, I am skeptical.

Jung, in my opinion, frequently rehearsed early memories, beginning, in 1913, with his self-analysis. I believe that having recovered certain memories which seemed to be significant, he mulled over and interpreted them and, by so doing, made them a part of his adult world. They were intellectualized and idealized. Later, whenever he returned to early childhood memories, these particular scenes and scenarios reappeared. According to Jaffé, when the octogenarian Jung began his collaborative work on *Memories, Dreams, Reflections*, he recovered memories that actually were fresh, and that had been repressed or forgotten. This, of course, is possible, but it is absolutely impossible to verify it. One way to recover old memories is to focus on particular events and scenes that are familiar and to broaden them out. Jung used this technique in dream analysis, and it can be applied to memory analysis as well. After exhausting all possible relevance to day residue in Jungian dream analysis, the technique calls for mythic associations and, very possibly Jung employed something of the sort when he indulged in memory recovery while writing the first two chapters of *Memories*.

Laufen and the Falls of the Rhine are the kind of place that would make a profound impression on the mind of a very young child. As one makes one's way down the highly civilized, well-kept trail, the falls, which had been inaudible and hidden, suddenly come into view, and one hears the roar. The wildness has been preserved, and also the romance. This place charmed the young English poet William Wordsworth and, a few years later, the thirteen-year-old John Ruskin. They have left us their vivid descriptions because the Rhine Falls were one of those spots in Europe that inspired the romantic movement. The place seems mysterious, as if concealing a great secret, but would one think so if one did not know of its literary associations? To some tourists it is simply pretty, and to many, especially North Americans, overrated. It is not really a falls at all, but a cataract. I also felt that it was slightly sinister, but I doubt that I would have had I not read Jung's *Memories, Dreams, Reflections*, which, indeed, I had brought with me as my guidebook for the visit. To the young Carl it was a place of danger, and he dwells much more on the frightening aspects of the falls than on their beauty.

Whether the falls are beautiful or frightening is in the eye of the beholder. When one is on the railroad bridge halfway across, it is very clear that they could be frightening to a young child. I first saw Niagara Falls when I was four, and I remember being in a raincoat on the *Maid of the Mist*, the roar of the falls and the spray, and with a feeling of anxiety and dis-ease as well as awe. But do I remember the actual experience itself as it actually was, and as I actually felt at the time? Or am I dredging up revised versions? As I think of this trivial incident in 1928, I recall being in a raincoat, and a green pennant labeled NIAGARA FALLS, which the family had for years. Doubtless, if I focused on this memory, other such details, long fogotten, might reappear in my memory. But am I remembering the incident itself, or memories of memories? I doubt that this highly subjective question can be answered. Another example is my recollection of the Pearl Harbor raid of December 7, 1941, when I was university age, which I have retraced and interpreted so many times in the years since that I cannot be sure at all of the original memories. At the very least, they have been altered simply by my telling of my war story.

Jung's memories of the Falls of the Rhine were unquestionably polluted by his later intellectualizing, in the course of which he mythologized them just as I have mythologized the Pearl Harbor raid. These are all reasons why introspection as a technique was abandoned by experimental psychologists. Be that as it may, the scenes of Jung's early childhood were certainly important to him in later years when he founded analytical psychology. Among the earliest of them are Laufen and the Falls of the Rhine. It is no ordinary place.

As one crosses the railroad bridge and faces west, one sees and hears the foaming, roiling, boiling Rhine below, the white water, and the black jagged rocks, one of them marked with a fluttering Swiss flag. The water roars down the cataract into a basin here. One feels the danger. If the guardrails were to give way and one fell, one would quickly be swept over the falls, dashed against the rocks, and killed.

There were accidents while Carl was the infant son of the pastor. He remembered at least one broken bleeding corpse, which the fishermen took to the laundry house, and the blood and water that streamed from the gutter when he eluded his mother and ran out to see. He remembered the burials, not all of which were of familiar villagers. He probably heard the adults talk about accidents and drownings.

Young children sometimes are acutely aware of death. Although I do not remember it, my mother told me that when I was very ill with scarlet fever, I became hysterical and shrieked for my parents to take a black crib out of the room. Was this an archetypal vision?

Van der Post draws contrasts between the still deep waters of Lake Constance usually shrouded in mists, and the ever-flowing Rhine. Except in the Alpine heights of Grisons where it rises, and at Rhine Falls, the Rhine flows calmly and majestically to the sea. According to Van der Post, early proximity to lake and river, underscored by his visit to Lake Constance when he was three and a half, convinced Jung that he must live near water. As a newly married young man with a growing family, he often gazed at Lake Zürich from hill-top Burghölzli and decided that they must live by the lakeshore. The lake evoked the collective unconscious in the depths of his psyche.

In retrospect, the octogenarian Jung shaped and formed a

childhood scenario sequence that began with his death anxieties because of the Falls as a zone of danger. These fears became incorporated into a pattern made up of other terrors occasioned by his confusion of Lord Jesus with the Jesuits who supposedly lurked in the neighborhood, and both with the demonic vision of an underground phallus king in a vivid dream. Shaped first into a story and then into a hermeneutic interpretation, the boyhood dream of the underground phallus king assumed enormous importance in later years, far more so than it probably had in his early childhood. In that way, Jung mythologized his early memories and made them the genesis of his doctrine of the collective unconscious. Employing the introspective technique, he made memories of the early childhood dream primary data in his adult efforts to work out his theory of the collective unconscious.

I think that the scenario he created is like a poem, a scene in a play, or an episode in a novel. It is here that his warning to us in the prologue is most appropriate. He tells us that he is not going to give us biography in the usual sense, but that he is going to weave a myth which, in his terms, means revelation of the archetypes of the collective unconscious.

The elements of this mythic scenario are (1) his impression of funerals, (2) his confusion of "Jesuit" with "Jesus," (3) the "child-eating" Jesus of his mother's bedtime prayer, and (4) the dream of the underground phallus king. Jung idealized and structured them into a sequential story, probably around the year 1927 when, as he mentions in *Memories, Dreams, Reflections*, he finally decided what the dream meant.

One aspect of this early childhood myth is the story of his mother's disappearance when he was around three and a half, and his strong sense of loss. She returned, of course, after a sabbatical from her unhappy marriage, during which she may have been in hospital in Basel. During her absence, he was cared for by a maiden aunt whom he disliked, but was warmly mothered by the young maid, probably a local teenager, and also cared for by his father, who did not desert him but who was "there for him," as would be said today. These were the elements of the subplot in his Rhine Falls myth.

In retrospect, he interpreted the events more or less as Biblical scholars do in exegesis and commentary. The meaning of the myth is that from then on woman symbolized unreliability to him and man reliability but weakness. Very probably the conscientious but unhappy father radiated insecurity and personal lack of confidence, and his own sense of failure. No doubt his work was his defense, possibly his evasion of life. He was one of those who, like Sinclair Lewis's George Babbitt, could lament, "I never did anything I wanted to do."

In retrospect Jung recalled fear of his mother because of her mysterious Personality Number Two, her weird comments to him yet apparently to herself, and her nocturnal strangeness, giving rise to eerie visions. These characteristics of his mother were particularly baffling because she was otherwise so conventional. In these ways Jung's parents framed the scenario of the dream of the underground king and made it seem all the more sinister.

Today, children are usually shielded from death, but in Jung's childhood it was ubiquitous. My parents, who were born during the late 1880s and early 1890s, often spoke of the early deaths of siblings and of their parents. In those days, most people died at home, and the undertakers came and prepared the corpse for burial. Many people died in the prime of life. My father lost his mother when he was eighteen; my mother had lost both of her parents by the time she was that age. From their stories, I had the impression, as a boy, that people of all ages were constantly dying all around my parents during their years of childhood and youth. In that way Jung, like almost all children in the nineteenth century and earlier, constantly heard about death, was aware that people whom he knew had vanished, and was acutely aware of his own mortality. Indeed, he experienced death far more than most children did because his father was a pastor, and funerals were as much a part of his business as of an undertaker's. The boy was taken to the funerals, and here he learned that people whom he knew had been laid in boxes and that the boxes were then lowered into the ground by the pallbearers in black frock coats, tall hats, and shiny boots. In that connection, he also heard his father say that someone called "Lord Jesus" had taken them to himself. What could that possibly mean to a child of three and a half to four?

With the somberly dressed villagers, Lord Jesus, and funerals so intertwined, it is no wonder that Jung totally misunderstood both his childhood prayer and the figure coming down the hill whom he took for "Jesuit/Jesus" coming for him.

Thinly disguised hostility is found in many nursery rhymes and lullabies; outlets, I think, for the anger and frustration of harassed mothers and other care-givers with dependents whom they are always expected to regard with forbearance and love no matter what they may honestly feel. Why is one of the most familiar lullabies "Rockabye, Baby"? Consider the words, "When the wind blows, the cradle will rock. When the bough breaks, the cradle will fall, and down will come cradle, baby, and all." An Afrikaans lullaby from South Africa goes: ". . . zimm bam bam, mommie's baby, twist his neck and hit him on his head, throw him in the ditch until he's dead."

The lullaby Jung's mother sang to him is familiar to most German-speaking people. "Spread out thy wings, Lord Jesus mild. And take to thee thy chick, thy child. If Satan would devour it. No harm shall overpower it. So let the angels sing." German mothers still sing it, even today.

Günther Looser reveals certain nuances in the Swiss dialect called Schweizertütsch that Jung spoke as a child, which are missed in translation or even in standard German. "And take to thee thy chick thy child," for instance, has double meaning both in German and English. Sometimes people say "I always take coffee," meaning that they drink it. In German *nimm* (from *einnehmen*) also means "to take," "to gather in," or "to swallow," "to eat." In high German the word *Küchlein* means "chick," as in "take to thee thy chick, thy child" but it is close to the Schweizertütsch word *chüchli* which means "little cakes" or "cookies."

The boy could have heard "Spread out thy wings, Lord Jesus mild, and eat thy cookie, thy child." Why? So Satan won't eat him first. Thus, while both Satan and Lord Jesus were cookie monsters, Lord Jesus was the one to be most feared because his mother, whose occasional eeriness frightened him, was asking Lord Jesus to eat him. The effect, I would add, might have been much the same as when the Afrikaander mother cheerfully sings, ". . . twist his neck and hit him on his head, throw him in the ditch until he's dead." Usually, of course, she knows that she does not mean a word of it, but there are days when she does! We now know that child abuse is very prevalent and always has been; that more than one child has been battered or killed by his or her own mother. A dog recognizes which is the strongest in will between his master and mistress, and so do children. The boy Carl knew that his mother was, by far, the stronger willed of his two parents, and that he had much more to fear from her than he did from his irritable but ineffectual father.

In part, Carl's distress as a child was because of language. In German, *Jesuit* and *Jesus* are pronounced "Yayzoot" and "Yayzoo," so that a misunderstanding that would not happen in English could easily happen in German. "Jeh-zwit" does not sound at all like "Jee-sus." The German-speaking boy confused them.

In *Memories, Dreams, Reflections*, Jung tells us that he overheard worried, agitated conversation between his father and neighboring colleagues about Jesuits. As in neighboring Germany, there was a Swiss *Kulturkampf* during the late nineteenth century. In Switzerland, it was aggravated by memories of the Sonderbund War of the 1840s, after which the Jesuits were expelled. They were blamed for having stirred the seven Catholic cantons into armed revolt against the confederation. Therefore, the appearance of Jesuits in a solidly Protestant Zürich canton meant trouble.

The three-and-a-half year old Carl, of course, knew nothing whatsoever about the politics of the day, much less what Catholics and Protestants were. He only knew people whom his father and his friends called "Yayzoot" were around, which made his father both angry and afraid. Not long after he overheard the conversation, while he was playing outside in the sand, he looked up to see a horrible sight. A black figure was coming down the hill, a man wearing women's clothes, and coming straight for him. It was "Yayzoot"! No wonder he bolted for the house, raced upstairs, and hid. Yet there is a curious gap in the story. How did he know that this was a "Yayzoot"?

About this time, the boy Carl had a strange dream, referred to as the dream of the underground phallus king. In the dream, he found himself in the tree-fringed meadow I have described, which stretches to the east of the tall *Pfarrhaus*. There he found his *Avernus*, a stone-dressed entrance to the underworld with steps leading down. He made his way down to find himself in a walled chamber; before him was a Roman arch and a green curtain of thick brocaded stuff. He pushed his way through to a stone-lined inner chamber with gutters at the side. A rich red carpet ran the length of the chamber down the center. There was a low platform and, on it, a golden throne. On the throne stood a huge, tall cylinder with a rounded head. A single eye gazed motionless at the ceiling. At that moment, he heard his mother's voice outside call "*Ja, sieh ihm an. Das ist der Menschenfresser!*" ("Yes, just look at him. That is the man-eater!")

The dream woke the boy up, drenched in sweat and terrified. It was a nightmare that mystified and haunted him the rest of his life, obviously a very important dream. In his own rather unconvincing explanation, he claims that he did not know that it was a penis even though he had one himself, and that, although the chamber reminded him of Mûnot Castle, no one would have taken a child there. Why was he so sure of that? In other words, Jung brushes off obvious, day-residue explanations for the dream which occur to me, and quickly leaps to far-fetched etymological and mythic explanations which he does not develop. He is too eager to show that this can only be an archetypal dream.

Jung's own interpretation is partially etymological, and also wrong. He argues that *phallus* is a Greek word which means "light," and that this explains the aura above the head of the penis. However, the Greek for "light" is not *phalos* but *pharos*. Even if it did mean "shining," "bright," I am bemused by his conclusion that "the phallus of the dream is a subterranean god 'not to be named.'" He adds the unlikely thought, "such it remained throughout my youth, reappearing whenever anyone spoke too emphatically about Lord Jesus" (Jung 1961, 13).

Jung does not explain how a complex and subtle etymological reference gave rise to an archetypal symbol in the dream of a three-and-a-half year old child. He also does not explain how the erect penis of the dream could be a subterranean god. It was certainly not that in the conscious mind of the child. However, as one compares this image with Jung's oft-repeated story of the solar phallus man, the argument is explicable if not convincing. Neither the mental patient nor the boy knew what they saw in the respective delusion and dream. It is rather that both images revealed themselves unbidden and incomprehensible, and with no reference whatsoever to anything in the life experience of patient and child. That, I would assume, is what Jung meant to say.

In his comments on the dream, Jung became both arrogant and dogmatic. He brusquely dismissed skeptics, calling them pollywogs who do not realize that the pond they are in is drying up. He dogmatically asserted that this was a dream that can be explained in no other way than as a revelation of the archetypes of the collective unconscious. He insisted that we accept it as such, as an article of faith.

This dream, and that of the solar phallus man, are important because they are among his chief proofs for the collective unconscious. Marie-Louise von Franz insists that it was the most important dream in Jung's life, his first encounter with the collective unconscious. She connects it with Eros and Jung's nine- and ten-year-old fantasies surrounding his manikin in the pencil box, which I will discuss later. Von Franz connected the phallus king in Jung's dream with symbolic phalluses that Greeks, Romans, and Etruscans sometimes placed on graves. They were symbols of future life. Rather improbably, she also links this idea to the "death of God" theme in *Thus Spake Zarathustra*, as Nietzsche's symbol of the secularism of modern Europe. She notes that Hermes was sometimes symbolized as a phallus in Greece. He conducted souls to the underworld. "This 'subterranean'. . . god image which appeared to him in his first dream marked his religious outlook for the rest of his life." The god image was not merely hidden but "alive in the depths of the grass-covered earth, in nature" (von Franz 1976, 26f.).

In "The Creative Phases in Jung's Life," (1972), Jaffé discussed the dream, referring to the "power, majesty, and numinosity" of the "phallic daimon." It is "a living, creative, and perceiving spirit dwelling in the dark recesses of the psyche." It is an ambivalent figure, simultaneously terrifying to the child and also awesome. The invisible voice of Carl's mother is also ambivalent. "Yes, just look at him. That is the man-eater!" On the one hand she invites the boy to really see the mysterious thing, and, at the same time, warns him that it is murderous. Jaffé thinks that "Her call seems to have the secret design of preventing her son's fateful encounter with the daimon." The mother herself is adoring and nurturant but she is also as dangerous as the underground phallus. "Moreover we know from the laws of dream events that the phallic daimon shows itself so threatening and terrifying only because it is denied, and not the other way round" (Jaffé 1972, 163f.).

The underground phallus king is "a subterranean god 'not to be named,'" (Jung 1961, 13), "the antagonist of the trusted, bright Lord Jesus," and he is "an unsought-after-frightful-revelation" (Jaffé 1972, 164). He is one and the same with the Lord Jesus who wears a golden crown and sits on a throne high in the sky beside the Father. They are not opposites. Instead, Lord Jesus/Phallus King, Christ/Lucifer, light/darkness, good/evil, and consciousness/unconscious are the same. The dream was Carl's "initiation into the realm of darkness," a harbinger of his later creativity because, in his scientific work, he focused on the dark aspect of the psyche.

As Frazer Boa remarked in a CBC Ideas program, Jung idealized this dream and, in the course of working over the memory trace undoubtedly altered it unintentionally and subconsciously. Around 1927, he concluded that he had seen a "ritual phallus." By then, however, he had intellectualized the dream. By the time Jung wrote about the dream in the first chapter of *Memories, Dreams, Reflections*, the dream, like the story of the solar phallus man, had become a personal myth. It is impossible to find a "pre-Jaffé" explanation, as Noll complains, nor for that matter recover with any confidence the original childhood dreams and visions which Jung used in his memoir. However, I disagree with both Stern and Noll that Jung had ulterior motives, and that the purpose of the revelation was to present himself as a prophet or "divine man." Instead, I think that Jung was sincerely engaged in a quest and convinced that he had unlocked great mysteries.

There are, however, simpler explanations. In Jungian dream analysis, those who would interpret a dream are advised to focus on the immediate explanations first, and not to turn to etymological, symbolic, and mythical interpretations until those having to do with day residue and the immediate circumstances of the dreamer's life have been thoroughly exhausted. As the dreamer, only Jung was qualified to comment. Only the dreamer knows the meaning of the dream. In this case, by his own admission, he did not begin to interpret it until his adult years, and arrived at his mythic and archetypal interpretation around 1927 when he read an article on ritual cannibalism. This is not proper Jungian dream analysis. By the time Jung had reached puberty, the dream, by his own admission, had become part of his conscious life and had been long pondered and worked over. Still, even conceding that, he is much too cavalier, skips over obvious explanations, and makes assumptions. What is given in *Memories, Dreams, Reflections* is remarkably incompetent Jungian dream analysis. Above all, he did not exhaust all possible personal explanations for the dream, but immediately leaped to the mythical and symbolic. He dismissed too quickly the possibility that the dream, after all, did actually stem from scenes and occurrences in his personal life when he was a child. Indeed, Freudian analysis would have been more appropriate, considering that this is a dream with obvious sexual connotations.

The Jungian analyst Satinover suggests that Carl may have been sexually abused by a Catholic priest. It is certainly a possibility. As is now known, homosexuality and pedophilia are, and probably always have been, widespread among Catholic priests. As a teenager, he was indeed sexually abused by "a man whom I always had trusted," as he mentioned in a letter to Freud. It could also have happened when he was a child. That might explain the dream.

He had the dream while he was perplexed by the confusion of "Jesuit" with "Jesus," as well as by the sinister words of the childhood prayer in which Lord Jesus seemed to be a cookie monster. He had also been frightened by the sudden appearance of the priest on the Dachsen Road. The underground, castle-like chamber with its red carpet and throne sound very much like illustrations in a nineteenth-century child's book of fairy tales. If not that, Laufen, now a restaurant, is a castle, and there is also the small castle of Wörth across the Rhine. His parents, aunt, or the maid might well have taken him to Münot, the imposing hill castle in Schaffhausen. I do not buy the dogmatic assertion that no one would have taken a child there. Why not? Jung dismissed all of these possibilities much too quickly in his eagerness for a mythic explanation.

Satinover's charge that Jung suffered sexual abuse by a Jesuit is at least possible, as is abuse by someone else in the neighborhood. Until recently, the prevalence of sexual abuse of children was minimized, and, indeed, as Jeffrey Moussaieff Masson showed, Freud appears to have falsified his own clear evidence of prevalent child abuse for fear of offending public opinion. That situation had not materially changed in Jung's later years. Indeed, there are still people who refuse to believe in such abuse, so deeply entrenched is the myth of childhood innocence. If a young child dreams of a penislike column, there could be sexual connotations. If, at the same time, the child is also terrified of Catholic priests, it is not unreasonable to suppose, as does Satinover, that the child may have been sexually abused by a priest. The myth of priestly innocence is another illusion that has been exploded in recent years.

The dream is still puzzling. What did his mother mean when she said, "Yes, just look at him. That is the man-eater!"? Jung never answered that question, and it is highly unlikely that it can be answered. However, it is much more probable that it relates to something in the boy's life in the then-and-there than to some symbolic or mythic revelation of the archetypes.

Three

The Manikin in the Pencil Box

Klein-Hüningen

In 1879, when Carl was four, the Basel consistory transferred his father to the Klein-Hüningen parish across the Rhine from the city and close to the German border. Then it was a tiny hamlet peopled by fishermen and their families, farmers, a few craftsmen and merchants, and one or two wealthy families. Now Klein-Hüningen is the Basel industrial zone. However, the old houses of Jung's boyhood survive in the neighborhood of the church. Now Dorfstrasse, the main street of the village, is the terminus of tram line #43, a half-hour ride from the center of Basel. Then it was at least a two-hour walk, and almost the same by carriage.

Old photographs in Paul Hugger's *Kleinhüningen* show a man with a cow in the center of the village, rustic peasants, stone-built homes, and the green cupola and steeple of the tall church towering over the village. The photographs also show open fields and hedgerows, clumps of trees, and scattered farm buildings. A map of Klein-Hüningen as it was in 1880 shows a typical Swiss Rhenish village with a population of a few hundred.

The church is impressive. Built in 1745, it evokes the milieu of the eighteenth century. It is surrounded by a high wall of masonry. Inside, it has a high pulpit and stained glass windows. The pastor was the parson, the most important person in the town. Much to Carl Jung's annoyance, he was called "Pastor's Carl" when he was a boy. Like the church at Laufen, that of Klein-Hüningen is remarkably tall and spacious. It gives the impression of being important and that the pastor was also important.

Past Klein-Hüningen to the west, the Rhine makes an abrupt swing northwest as it continues its way through Germany to Holland and the North Sea. The Alsace lies on the left bank and Baden on the right. The Alsace was French when Jung's grandfather came from Paris to Basel. After the Franco-German War of 1870, it was a province of the German Empire. It is German-speaking.

The River Wiese flows into the Rhine at Klein-Hüningen. It flooded, causing some loss of life, soon after the Jungs settled in the village.

Carl's boyhood world was rustic. It was a countryside of open fields, stands of tall oak, ash, and linden trees, a view of the Black Forest to the southeast, Basel Cathedral and the bridge spanning the Rhine to the northeast, the Rhine, and the rolling hills of the Alsace across the Rhine.

As a boy, Carl loved to roam alone through the countryside, to make his way down to the Rhine or hike in the Black Forest. National formalities were ignored, and Germans and Swiss constantly roamed back and forth over the border. Basel is now a salient surrounded by Germany on two sides, with France to the west on the third. In Jung's boyhood it was surrounded by Germany on all three sides.

Carl's early impressions of nature were not idyllic, but of a battleground in which even plant life was engaged in a ruthless, competitive struggle to survive. The boy Jung's early view of nature was not romantic like that of Wordsworth, but, like Tennyson's law of tooth and fang, wholly consistent with the Darwinian view, which he learned about much later.

This was because, unlike the romantic poets, Jung studied nature at close hand and discovered her savagery. This was particularly true during the period of his life that I call his half-sabbatical. At age thirteen, using a fall and head injury as an excuse, he shirked school and daydreamed around the Swiss countryside for a term, a time-out period of his childhood that actually became more important in his development than anything he learned in the Basel Humanistisch Gymnasium.

> What had led me astray during the crisis was my passion for being alone, my delight in solitude. Nature seemed to me full of wonders, and I wanted to steep myself in them. Every stone, every plant, every single thing seemed alive and indescribably

marvelous. I immersed myself in nature, crawled, as it were, into the very essence of nature and away from the whole human world. (Jung 1961, 32)

As a boy, Jung secretly called nature "God's World," a pious label easily misunderstood. He did not mean by it the benevolent realm of the Anglican hymn that praises "all creatures great and small," nor an idyllic Wordsworthian realm of dancing daffodils. Instead, because the boy studied nature closely, he discovered how ruthlessly ants make war, how savagely predators kill their prey, and how plants bound for good or ill to their places struggled for sunlight. Thus, while he saw God in nature, it was not the romantic vision of a misty Chinese landscape. The countryside around Klein-Hüningen is gentle like the English countryside and, seen from a discreet distance, one is charmed by it. At close hand, it is as savage as the African jungle. Jung discovered here the harshness and hardness of God.

The boys at school teased Carl, and, to his great chagrin, called him "Father Abraham." He could not understand why at first, but then realized that it did not quite mean the same thing as when rustic school chums in Klein-Hüningen called him "Pastor's Carl." The boys in Basel meant that he was a country bumpkin, and also that he was different. How he understood that from the term "Father Abraham" is not at all clear to me, but what follows in his memoirs is mystical, if not patriarchal or prophetic.

Until age eleven, when he entered gymnasium, Carl had lived in country villages with rare excursions to Basel, the one city of his early years. He now became aware of the existence of two distinct worlds. The boy Carl realized the contrast between the two realities, and called that of nature, "God's World." He did not name the other, but it could have been called, as with Augustine, "The City of Man." Unlike the neoromantics, Carl was not at all sympathetic to the latter, and certainly not to the positivist realm of scientific and technological achievement. Basel was alien to him, and loathsome, not least because the Preiswerks lived there and he did not like his mother's relatives. He also hated school. That, too, was of that other world with its haughty boys, their smug elders, noise, bustle, and, though he did not mention this, the expanding industrial wasteland of Klein-Hüningen, which he was forced to walk through every day to and from school.

"God's World" was of a different order, "filled with secret meaning." Not an Eden or Arcady: to the contrary, there was ruthlessness and heartless cruelty in nature, an unrelenting struggle for existence. He was impressed by the "sorrowful, lost look of the cows, and in the resigned eyes of horses." He noted that people were like animals, "and seemed as unconscious as they." But Carl saw that people, animals, growing things, rocks, and stars all dwell "in a unified cosmos, in God's World, in an eternity where everything is already born and everything has already died" (Jung 1961, 66f.).

Jung is very eloquent here. But are these the thoughts of Carl, aged eleven or twelve, or of a wise old man in the last years of a long life? I can recall similar thoughts of my own at eleven or twelve. I remember gazing at a starry sky in deeper awe than I have ever experienced in my adult years, and asking my father, "Where do they all end?" Then, when I was sixteen, I became interested in astronomy, learned the constellations, and read all I could find on the subject in the library. I became very knowledgeable, but also experienced a sense of loss. Now, when I looked up, I identified Perseus, Orion, the Southern Cross. I knew the speed of light and the various current theories about the origins of the universe. But with this information, I had dropped the cosmos into the everyday world and lost the naive sense of awe I had first felt when I gazed up into the starry sky and wondered where it all ended.

But I can still remember my youthful awe of what Jung called "God's World." If I can do that, Jung certainly could have done so as well when he wrote *Memories, Dreams, Reflections*. There is thus probably a core of truth in his memories of childhood, however much he intellectualized them later. The same is probably true of his historical observations.

North America is, historically, rather thin. I discovered this when I lived in England. There, one is not only constantly aware of history, but of prehistory. I lived in Coventry. Every day I went to Coventry Technical College, where I worked, past the spot where Peeping Tom supposedly was struck blind when Lady Godiva made her famous ride. The college stands at the Butts, where medieval archers practiced. The ruins of the old Coventry Cathedral are medieval, as is the castle and cathedral at nearby Warwick. An hour's drive, and one reaches the prehistoric Rollright Stones.

Jung was privileged to grow up in Europe, in sight of the Black Forest, in a land marched over by armies during the Thirty Years War, and, later, the Napoleonic Wars. He lived where there had been lords and ladies, knights, princes, dukes, and their men-at-arms. He lived in a manse that had once been the home of a titled aristocrat. To a European child, history is real and omnipresent. It is deep, and in its own way, as awesome as the starry sky. Anyone who has lived there knows this feeling, this awesome grasp of the reality of history.

The neighborhood of Klein-Hüningen was not only a natural battlefield, but a battlefield of nations. The ruins of the French frontier fortress of Huninque lay just across the Rhine, a reminder that mighty armies had crossed the river to march to and from great battles.

The French built this powerful fort during the reign of Louis XIV, and, by so doing, attracted hostile armies into the neighborhood (Hugger 1984, 13). The Austrians invaded and laid siege to the Huninque redoubt during the War of Spanish Succession at the beginning of the eighteenth century. During the Napoleonic Wars, a French army crossed the Rhine near Klein-Hüningen and later recrossed in retreat. Klein-Hüningen's great crisis was in the year 1814, when Huninque shelled it. Round shot and grenades smashed houses and the chancel of the Reformed Church. There was more trouble the next year. Napoleon was defeated at Waterloo, but Huninque did not surrender until the end of August. An allied army of Austrians, Russians, and Swiss laid siege, and Klein-Hüningen was again in war. When Jung was a boy, there would have been elderly people in the village who remembered these events (Hugger 1984, 13).

During Jung's boyhood, Basel entered the industrial revolution and the modern age. Klein-Hüningen was affected. I am curious that Jung makes no mention of the wealthy Clavels of Lyons who had a summer home built in Klein-Hüningen during the 1880s. By 1900, their chemical firm had become CIBA, one of the major Basel chemical corporations. By then, Klein-Basel across the Rhine from Basel had become an ugly sprawl of factories. Jung never mentions them, but must have hated them. They are probably a reason for his lifelong antipathy to materialism and technology.

"I no longer remember our move to Klein-Hüningen, near Basel, in 1879," Jung writes. Klein-Hüningen was then a collection of around fifty houses along the Klybeckstrasse, which was an extension of the Rheinweg. The latter is the road to the Basel bridgehead. Very few of the old houses survive, but the Swiss Reformed Church does, and also the parsonage. So does the old *stube* (beer hall) between them. One expects to find the parsonage next to the church, but it was not. The street that runs in front of the church and parsonage is now called Dorfstrasse, or Village Street. Now it is paved, with sidewalks. Then it was a dirt road, dusty in summer, a quagmire of mud in wet winters and spring, and constantly perfumed with horse manure. The center of Carl's world was the parsonage, the garden, and behind it a wall, which still survived when I visited the parsonage, but is probably gone now because the church is in debt and is selling off part of the property. When I saw it, there was a tangle of wild brush behind it, and a boat-building shop with a galvanized iron roof a few feet further on. It, or its predecessor, was there when Carl was a young man, but probably not when he was a boy. Then the open fields and meadows stretched in all directions and the Rhine was in full view.

Today the parsonage is subdivided into apartments, the largest of which was the home of Dr. Klein Anton, a chemist with CIBA Geigy of Klein-Hüningen and his wife Barbara Stuwe-Anton when I was last in Klein-Hüningen. She was the part-time pastor of what was Paul Jung's church.

The parsonage is imposing. It is three stories high with an attic. At the southern end of the attic there are cross beams. Young Carl hid a yellow pencil box, of which more later, on one of them. He was eight or nine then. When Carl was a boy, it was very much a dark attic where he often hid from his quarreling parents. The parsonage is situated north and south along Dorfstrasse. From the road it presents a typical example of eighteenth-century architecture. It was built for a German aristocrat in 1745. It has a mansard roof, shuttered windows, two on each side of the door on the first floor, and two smaller windows above. The window frames, shutters, and door are now dull red, but were probably darker in Jung's boyhood. The house is of stone and painted cream or ivory, as is the church.

That was a surprise. I had expected something sombre. The appearance of both the house and church is rather cheerful. The *stube* between them is grey. This is where Carl's father or one of the deacons bought the sour wine that so repelled Carl at his first communion.

The house has a hidden half-basement without any means of access. There are two windows on the opposite sides. Looking in, one can see an earthen floor at window level, and some rubbish. Why are there windows in a room which has no means of entrance? The effect is a bit eerie.

The parlor on the second floor is large and bright, a rather cheerful room today. Indeed, the house itself is quite elegant, as Jung acknowledged. The present occupants find it very comfortable. Dr. Anton, who has considerable interest in Jung, showed me the porch from which Carl and his father gazed, in 1883, at the green sunset. Jung's father told him the sky was green because of volcanic dust from the explosion of Krakatoa between Sumatra and Java in the far away Dutch East Indies on the other side of the world. One is impressed with the parsonage, church, and their surroundings, which still retain their old charm. The house was too big for the impoverished Jungs, however, and they closed off many of the rooms.

As a boy, Jung was fascinated by a closed-off parlor.

> Here all the furniture was good, and old paintings hung on the walls. I particularly remember an Italian painting of David and Goliath. It was a mirror copy from the workshop of Guido Reni; the original hangs in the Louvre. How it came into our family I do not know. There was another old painting in that room which now hangs in my son's house: a landscape of Basel dating from the early nineteenth century. Often I would steal into that dark, sequestered room and sit for hours in front of the pictures, gazing at all this beauty. It was the only beautiful thing I knew. (Jung 1961, 16)

My visit to Klein-Hüningen was on a Sunday, and I attended the ten o'clock service. The bells in the round green belfry chimed, and I followed the worshippers in. The interior of the church is plain, but by no means drab or dreary. Indeed, the church building itself and its interior are both rather bright. There is a high pulpit, and rows of pews. The services are now conducted at floor level. There are usually from thirty to fifty in the congregation, most of them elderly.

The service is simple. It begins with a hymn which the congregation sings while seated. There are no litanies or responsive readings, but prayers and a twenty-minute sermon. After the sermon, the pastor leads the congregation in The Lord's Prayer. The pastor then recesses and goes to a small gatehouse, and the people mill about outside and chat with one another.

Carl hated the church services, and, from his comments in *Memories, Dreams, Reflections*, one suspects that they were much longer than now, the sermon especially. He does not identify his father's theological position, but the Evangelical Reformed Church of that day was much influenced by Adolf Harnack, especially during the 1880s and 1990s. Harnack was a liberal Protestant who thought that creeds and dogmas should be simplified.

In his memoirs, Jung gives the impression that his father was a failure, that he had no spiritual vocation, and that his ministry was unsuccessful. Jung recalled his father's nostalgia for his student days, his abandonment of his linguistic studies which had earned him a doctorate, and his irritability. However, Henri Ellenberger met an elderly woman who recalled Pastor Jung's warmth and friendliness, his good humor, kindliness, and generosity. She also recalled his powerful sermons. Jung makes much of his father's irritability at home, but no man is ever a hero to his own family. Jung himself was very difficult at home, as his son told me. Carl may have inherited his father's quick temper and his tendency to go into rages. Paul Jung had a very long pastorate, and did a great deal of good, as his son acknowledges. The mere fact that Paul Jung did not demand that his son attend church and that he tolerated his rejection of the communion service as well as his youthful theological heresies suggests that Jung's father was unusually liberal for the times. Pastor Jung's long years of service to the Basel mental hospital show that he was a man with a strong social conscience. Although Carl Jung appears to have regarded his father as an intellectual lightweight, he seems to have been an effective pastor. He was also respected at the university and, indeed, he seems to have secured his son's scholarship on the strength of his own reputation.

Carl's father apparently related quite well to his rustic parishioners. In later years, Carl recalled their tall black hats, long dark frock coats, and shiny boots on Sunday mornings and at funerals. He did not recall his father's parishioners in their work clothes or when they were relaxed and at play. They had their folk festivals and times of fun. That there were such times is evident from Paul Hugger's *Kleinhüningen.* Jung mentioned costumed revels in Basel, but never in his memoirs, in which he mostly recalled his solitary times of inner reflection. One easily imagines him sitting on the parsonage wall, or on the famous stone, which the present occupants have looked for but not found. One imagines him wandering about the neighborhood, and his solitary hours in the attic with his secret pencil box. From Klein-Hüningen one can see the Black Forest, Basel and its bridges in the distance, and, of course, the Rhine itself with its cargo boats and the constant sounds and sights of busy river traffic. Basel is Switzerland's nearest equivalent to a seaport, her window on the world. One easily imagines how the sights and sounds of the Rhine found their way into the deepest recesses of Jung's psyche.

In their later years, people often recall their days of childhood and youth through a golden haze. We are all very selective and, by being so, create private myths. Extraverted people recall people and social events, the parties they went to, the football matches, playmates, and old enemies. Their recollections are usually social. Introverts are more like cats. They are chiefly nostalgic for places and scenes, for the way places looked, for smells, and sounds. They remember sights; they also remember their own inner thoughts and feelings as children. Carl Jung's recollections were typically introverted. Chiefly, he recalls his fantasies and visions, his inner thoughts and reflections. Beyond that, he recalls childhood scenes that included people like his parents, but in which others were chiefly actors in the private theater of his mind. Like many introverts, Carl was usually a spectator, much inclined to view life from afar. His recollections are made up of impressions and sense experiences, fantasies, dreams, and visions. His landscapes are filled with the plants and animals, rivers, lakes, and mountains of "God's World." The people in his memories are mainly stage props, like the trees, houses, and animals.

There is far less recollection of outward events than of solitary moments of contemplation and reflection.

The Rheinweg, the long road to Basel, was an important part of young Carl's world. Today, his father's church and parsonage are only a few blocks away from the terminus of a tram line from Basel. It is a half-hour ride from the center of the city. Then, Basel was a long walk away. I found that I was not up to it. It would have taken me an hour and a half, at least. Carl walked it every day from the age of eleven until he was twenty-one. He had to be up before dawn to get to school on time, and it would be late afternoon before he finally reached home again. Sometimes he made the walk with at least one schoolmate. Frequently, he was alone. He often arrived at school with wet socks, soaked through with rain or snow.

Even so, it was probably a pleasant experience on warm sunny days, far more so than being either at school or at home where he had to cope with people. This part of Switzerland has a rather mild climate. There is little snow in winter, and the summers are cool. It is beautiful. To the left, the wooded hills of Germany are always in view. Ahead, as one sets out from Klein-Hüningen, one sees the graceful spire of the cathedral on a high bluff; to the right across the Rhine is the fortress of Huninque. The boy walked along the bank of the broad, grey Rhine, which was then clean and unpolluted. In the distance was the Black Forest.

At the Basel Bridge, with its cantonal flags and gargoyle with tongue sticking out at Klein Basel, Carl crossed the Rhine on the one bridge that spanned the river at the time. In those days, the bridge was partly of wood. On the Basel side, he turned left and climbed Augustinegasse. On either side of the narrow brick road are late medieval and Renaissance houses; one dates back to 1472. They are all very charming and picturesque, living confirmation of history. The brick road leads to the Münsterplatz [cathedral square], famous throughout Europe for its exact proportions. There, the boy passed the portals of the red sandstone cathedral with its mythic sculpture of St. George spearing the dragon. Built by Emperor Henry II in 1039, it is one of the oldest cathedrals in Europe.

We know that the scenes of this daily walk made a profound impression on Carl Jung. In later years, he realized that his vision of the archetypes of the collective unconscious owed much to these long, apparently boring, daily walks to and from school, five days a week. They gave him much time to reflect. The sheer beauty of the familiar scenery made a deep impact on his soul. It was a countryside which he loved in a Germanic land that was steeped in history. It was a very rich world for a young boy to grow up in, even though his clothes were patched and his shoes were old and worn.

The Manikin in the Pencil Box

Jung was an only child until the age of nine. Even then, the age difference between him and his sister Gertrude (Trudi) meant that both children actually grew up as only children. There were playmates his age in Klein-Hüningen, but he felt ill at ease at school, where many of the boys came from wealthy homes. He was often alone, lost in the reveries of his private world. He later recalled, "The influence of this wider world, this world which contained others besides my parents, seemed to me dubious if not altogether suspect and, in some obscure way, hostile" (Jung 1961, 19).

He loved his solitary moments most, and, during the years of his childhood, when he was eight, nine, and ten, constantly daydreamed. He was particularly fond of a stone embedded in a slope near an old wall. He often sat on it in ruminative moods. "I am sitting on top of this stone and it is underneath," he said to himself. In his imagination, the stone said, "I am lying here on this slope and he is sitting on top of me." The question rose in Carl's mind, "Am I the one who is sitting on the stone, or am I the stone on which *he* is sitting?" The question fascinated him (Jung 1961, 20). Was he Carl or the stone? (This question, the fact that he could seriously doubt whether he was a stone or himself, has led Winnicott to diagnose childhood schizophrenia.) He returned to the slope thirty years later. "I was a married man, had children, a house, a place in the world, and a head full of ideas and plans," he wrote, "and suddenly I was again the child who had kindled a fire full of secret significance . . ." (Jung 1961, 20).

> [I] sat down on a stone without knowing whether it was I or I was it. I thought suddenly of my life in Zürich, and it seemed alien to me, like news from some remote world and time. This was frightening, for the world of my childhood in which I had

just become absorbed was *eternal*, and I had been wrenched away from it and had fallen into a time that continued to roll onward, moving farther and farther away (Jung 1961, 20).

Like the underground phallus dream of his infancy, the day-dream of the stone on the slope was a revelation. "I have never forgotten that moment," he recalled, "for it illuminated in a flash of lightning the quality of eternity in my childhood" (Jung 1961, 20f.).

When Carl was nine, he carved a little man on the end of a ruler and painted him with black ink. The manikin was dressed in a long frock coat and a tall hat. Carl sawed the little figure from the end of the ruler and deposited him in a bed which he made for him in a yellow varnished pencil box. He gave him a little blanket and also a stone which he had picked up on the bank of the Rhine. The stone was black, and he painted half of it grey with water color. Then he crept up to the attic, which was *streng verboten* as the floors were rotten due to woodworm. He hid the pencil box on the top of a beam. Thereafter, for about a year, he would steal up to the attic from time to time and give his little friend messages written on tiny scrolls. He particularly liked visiting him when his parents quarreled, or when his mother was ill and took to her bed. The very thought of the manikin in the pencil box made him feel an inner peace and security.

He had forgotten about the manikin by the time he was eleven, but suddenly remembered him again many years later when he was in the British Museum. There he saw a depiction of a Greek deity called Telesphorus reading from a scroll to Hermes, the messenger of the gods who is also the psy-chopomp who accompanies the souls of the dead into the un-derworld. Suddenly he remembered his long forgotten manikin and, at that moment, realized that the fantasy was of more than personal significance. Like the dream of the under-ground phallus, it had been a disclosure of an impersonal di-mension of psyche.

Three secrets in Jung's childhood were the dream of the phallus, the feeling of dread he felt when he once saw the black-robed Jesuit whom he confused with Jesus, and the manikin with the black stone. These secrets were very important to him, absorbing, but for reasons he could not fathom until much later.

The boy also loved his solitary nature rambles around the Swiss countryside:

> Nature seemed to me full of wonders, and I wanted to steep myself in them. Every stone, every plant, every single thing seemed alive and indescribably marvellous. I immersed myself in nature, crawled, as it were, into the very essence of nature and away from the whole human world. (Jung 1961, 32)

The Gymnasium Student

During the spring of 1886, at age eleven, Jung began his secondary education at the Basel Humanistisch Gymnasium which is located across the square from the cathedral. It is a dark grey windowless pile that one would not guess was a school unless told. As with many European urban schools, the outer appearance is grim. There is no schoolyard, and, from the outside, the school looks like an old office building.

In German-speaking countries, the gymnasium corresponds to junior high school and high school in the American and Canadian systems. The students are between eleven and eighteen. In Jung's day in Switzerland, education was free and compulsory up to the age of sixteen. It was also classical in type, and segregated by sexes. Boys were taught by men and girls by women. The curriculum emphasized Latin and Greek, in the first of which Jung excelled. He also did well in German literature and French. He was mediocre or poor in everything else, especially mathematics, his worst subject. He hated physical education and was bored by religious knowledge. He did so poorly in drawing that he was excused from the class. Pedagogy was authoritarian: the big pitcher-little mug system. The pupils sat in rigid rows at their desks and were encouraged to be docile and compliant. Jung, who had a mind of his own, was often in trouble.

Passing grades were 1, 2, or 3 for excellent, good, or average. On one of his surviving report cards, Carl had a 1 in Latin and a 3 in mathematics. His other grades are 1s and 2s. Although he recalled being a dunce at school, his grades were rather good.

In *Memories, Dreams, Reflections*, he recalled that he was ill at ease among his schoolmates, embarrassed because of his drab clothes and his obvious poverty compared to so many of his classmates. Some of them came from wealthy families, lived in elegant mansions, and their fathers owned fine teams of horses and magnificent carriages. What is more, some of his privileged schoolmates had been to the Alps, and a few had even been to the seaside.

Far from being timid or shy, Jung was usually in trouble. He was often faulted for deportment. His work seems to have been uneven. He occasionally produced brilliant essays that aroused the suspicions of the masters. He recalled one such occasion in the BBC interview with John Freeman in 1960. His schoolmaster accused him of cheating. "Jung, you are a liar!" "And then I got mad, and if I had had a knife it would not have gone well with him if I met him at night." Jung wryly added that "whenever anything went wrong it was always assumed that I was at the bottom of it." Most of his anecdotes of his schooldays end with, "And then I got mad!" Into old age, Jung was famous for his stormy rages. According to Paul Stern, he once bodily threw analyst Jolande Jacoby down a flight of stairs. Those, like Aniela Jaffé, who worked with Jung became accustomed to his rages and patiently waited them out with remarkable good humor. Recalling his father's irritability, and his paternal grandfather's as well, one supposes that the quick temper was a family trait.

In the BBC interview with John Freeman, Jung gleefully told what he did when a gang of boys waylaid him. He grabbed one of them, swung him around, and knocked down the rest. Tall and strong, Carl could always take care of himself. His boyhood friend, Albert Oeri, recalls his pranks and how Carl despised sissies. He seems to have been a fairly normal, robust boy with, however, an unusually sensitive inner life and an exceptionally deep fondness for nature.

For the most part, Jung recalled this latter side when he wrote *Memories, Dreams, Reflections*. The externals of his life did not interest him. Consequently, the reader necessarily gets an unbalanced picture of him as a boy: the impression that he was a daydreaming, social misfit who did poorly in school. Oeri's memories of him were not like this at all, save for one isolated incident at Laufen.

Both boys were around four when Oeri's parents brought Albert with them on a family visit. The parents hoped that Albert and Carl would play together, but Carl ignored Albert completely and was wholly absorbed in a little bowling game. Albert, who was used to the rough and tumble of a nursery full of active children, did not know what to make of Carl and thought him a monster. Some clinicians regard the incident as evidence of childhood schizophrenia, but to me, it seems typical of the only child. Carl was quite sociable among his rustic schoolmates in Klein-Hüningen, and, when he went to school in Basel, he had friends who were mostly country boys like himself. In other moods, Carl joined in pranks with other boys. Oeri particularly remembers Carl's mischief and his loud laugh. Speaking his Swiss-German country dialect, Carl was a typical country boy of the late nineteenth century, good natured and fun-loving much of the time, and often mischievous. He was something of a Swiss Huck Finn, who lived among trees, brooks, the river, fields and forests, animals and birds.

Jung recorded only three early dreams in detail. One was the dream of the underground phallus king. He mentioned a few other early dreams, from when he was around eight or nine, but only in passing. In one he saw a tiny ball in the distance which grew huge as it approached. In another, birds sitting on telegraph wires also grew monstrous.

Among the strangest of his childhood psychic experiences was an apparition, which floated from his mother's room, a ghostly form with neck and head. The head detached from the neck and floated ahead of it like a little moon. A second head detached from the first and so on seven times. Jung does not say more, but leaves us to wonder if it was a dream, a hypnagogic or hypnopompic experience, or a hallucination.

As for his daytime inner life, he mostly recalled his love of nature, his rambles in the countryside, and his close observations of "God's World." As mentioned previously, the latter was not an idyllic order, but a ruthless battleground in which animals and insects fed on one another, and in which the apparent beauty of blossom and butterfly was accompanied by ruthlessness. From these observations of nature, he derived profound impressions of a harsh divinity underlying nature. As a teenager, he was deeply preoccupied with an inner religious struggle inspired by his disenchantment with conventional piety coupled with profound faith in the grace of God experienced in the context of awesome cruelty.

As a boy, Jung appeared to be contemplative to an exceptional degree. If we can believe *Memories, Dreams, Reflections*, he was a young philosopher. But some of his thoughts seem rather sophisticated for a twelve- and thirteen-year-old.

Jung's poor mathematical skills were by no means unusual. He probably had a learning disability in that area. Oeri attributed Jung's poor mathematical performance to heredity. His maternal grandfather, Samuel Preiswerk, was notoriously poor at handling figures. Fortunately, neither his parents or his teachers made too much of his weaknesses, and, in any case, he did well enough in math to pass.

For Carl, however, math was misery.

> Mathematics classes became sheer terror and torture to me. Other subjects I found easy; and as, thanks to my good visual memory, I contrived for a long while to swindle my way through mathematics, I usually had good marks. But my fear of failure and my sense of smallness in face of the vast world around me created in me not only a dislike but a kind of silent despair which completely ruined school for me. (Jung 1961, 29)

Less explicable was his failure at drawing. Jung had a natural talent for the graphic arts, as can be seen from his mandala drawings many years later as well as his work in sculpture. However, he did very poorly in drawing class, so much so that the teachers gave up on him.

> . . . I was forced to copy prints of Greek gods with sightless eyes, and when that wouldn't go properly the teacher obviously thought I needed something more naturalistic and set before me the picture of a goat's head. This assignment I failed completely, and that was the end of my drawing classes. (Jung 1961, 29)

But during this same time, Jung was spending much of his spare time drawing battle scenes in scribblers, elaborate pictures of castles under siege, naval battles, and the like. He also liked to do Rorschach tests of his own devising: he blotted notebooks and interpreted the blots. From his Laufen days, when his mother showed him pictures of Greek and Hindu gods in *Orbis Pictus*, Carl was fascinated with mythology. He loved Greek and Latin literature and did well in both. When he was seventeen, archaeology and mythology were his favorite subjects. He studied both on his own.

A major incident of Jung's boyhood was an accident that happened during the early summer of 1887 when he was twelve.

> It was twelve o'clock, and the morning classes were over. Suddenly another boy gave me a shove that knocked me off my feet. I fell, striking my head against the curbstone so hard that I almost lost consciousness. For about half an hour afterward I was a little dazed. At the moment I felt the blow the thought flashed through my mind: "Now you won't have to go to school any more." I was only half unconscious, but I remained lying there a few moments longer than was strictly necessary, chiefly in order to avenge myself on my assailant. Then people picked me up and took me to a house nearby, where two elderly spinster aunts lived. (Jung 1961, 30)

For the next six months, Carl used fainting spells as an excuse to avoid school.

> I was free, could dream for hours, be anywhere I liked, in the woods or by the water, or draw. I resumed my battle pictures and furious scenes of war, of old castles that were being assaulted or burned, or drew page upon page of caricatures. . . .
>
> Above all, I was able to plunge into the world of the mysterious. To that realm belonged trees, a pool, the swamp, stones and animals, and my father's library. But I was growing more and more away from the world, and had all the while faint pangs of conscience. I frittered away my time with loafing, collecting, reading, and playing. But I did not feel any happier for it; I had the obscure feeling that I was fleeing from myself. (Jung 1961, 30f.)

Naturally, Carl's parents were both bewildered and worried. They consulted several physicians and also sent Carl to the city of Winterhus on holiday. Carl liked the railroad station there and also enjoyed his holiday, but when he came home, everything was as it had been before. One physician thought it was epilepsy, and, knowing that it was not, Carl laughed to himself at such nonsense. One day, however, he hid behind shrubs and eavesdropped on his father's conversation with a visitor.

"And how is your son?" the friend asked. "Ah, that's a sad business," his father said. "The doctors no longer know what is wrong with him. They think it may be epilepsy. It would be dreadful if he were incurable. I have lost what little I had, and what will become of the boy if he cannot earn his own living?"

Carl was shocked back to reality. "Why, then," he told himself, "I must get to work!" (Jung 1961, 31).

What followed was a tour de force. At that moment Carl decided to end his half sabbatical, leave his utopian dreamworld, and make himself get back to his studies and to school. He crept into his father's study and took out his Latin grammar. He began to study with earnest concentration. After ten minutes he had a fainting fit and nearly fell off his chair. But he would not let himself stop. Instead, he studied on and, after a few minutes, felt better. He went on. Fifteen minutes later he had another attack. "And now you must really get to work!" he told himself. A half hour later he had a third attack, the worst yet. Again he stuck it out. He worked another hour. At the end of that time he felt better than he had in months, had no more fits, and the deep satisfaction that he had cured himself. The attacks never recurred again. Soon after, Carl went back to school. Apparently, the attacks had been a neurotic manifestation (Jung 1961, 31f.).

As a teenager, he was very preoccupied with his own interests. These were mostly philosophical. His father's slim library was impoverished in that area, but did include Krug's *Philosophical Dictionary*, which is a formidable work. It also included Biedermeyer's theological study, which Carl read very critically. At his mother's suggestion he read Goethe's *Faust* (Jung 1961, 56, 60, 61).

Personalities One and Two

When he was very young, Carl became aware of an eerie side to his mother's personality that sometimes frightened him. He later became aware of another personality within himself. He gave it the prosaic label, Personality Number Two. Personality Number One was the Swiss schoolboy, his everyday self; Personality Number Two was a wise old man of the eighteenth century, not a fantasy figure created by his imagination, but, to him, a reality.

Just what Jung meant by Personality Number Two is difficult to grasp. He only speaks of it in *Memories, Dreams, Reflections*, and, although he insists that everyone has a Personality Number Two, he only discusses it in his mother and in
himself. According to Jung, he became aware of his own Number Two Personality following a trivial incident at Lake
Lucerne when he was twelve.

The family was visiting wealthy friends there and Carl and
another boy were allowed to paddle on the lake in a *waidling*,
a gondola-like boat, best steered if one stands by the tiller in
the stern. Carl was doing just that when the portly host an-
grily whistled him ashore and gave him a severe dressing down
for doing something so dangerous.

Carl was offended. He wrote: "I was seized by rage that this
fat, ignorant boor should dare to insult ME!" He went off an-
grily until it occurred to him that he was just a schoolboy and
not important. Later, however, he became obsessed with the
thought that there was another person in himself who *was* important. This other was an eighteenth-century gentleman who
wore buckled shoes and a powdered wig, and who rode in a
great coach called a fly, with high, concave rear wheels between which a box was suspended on springs and leather
thongs. The image was inspired by something he actually had
seen just a short time before. A horse-drawn antique green
coach had come rumbling out of the Black Forest one day and
been driven past Klein-Hüningen, where Carl had had a good
look at it. Also, he had noticed the terra-cotta figurine of a Dr.
Stückelberger about this time, a famous local Basel personality of the eighteenth century about whom colorful anecdotes
still circulated. About that time, he took to writing "1786" instead of "1886" on some of his themes at school and feeling
nostalgic as he did so.

None of this was remarkable as fantasy. Carl, however, believed in the reality of Personality Number Two, as he believed
in his identity with the stone near the parsonage wall on which
he had sat ruminating a year or so before. For that reason, clinical readers of *Memories, Dreams, Reflections*, such as F. Winnicott and Stern, diagnosed childhood schizophrenia.

Anticipating such a diagnosis, Jung firmly denied that his
Personality Number Two was dissociation, split personality,
or any other pathological condition. However, his denial is not

convincing to most students of Jung, including analysts and other psychologists and psychiatrists who respect him. The impression that he suffered from psychotic tendencies of some kind is deepened by his comment in *Memories, Dreams, Reflections* that "the Other [Personality Number Two] . . . knew God as a hidden, personal, and, at the same time, suprapersonal secret," and that, for Personality Number Two, "nothing separated man from God; indeed, it was as though the human mind looked down upon Creation simultaneously with God" (Jung 1961, 45).

Noll reminds us of the eccentricity of old Samuel Preiswerk, Jung's maternal grandfather, who thought that he was surrounded by a swarm of spirits. They could be frightened off, he thought, if someone stood behind him. Therefore, as a girl, Jung's mother Emilie had to stand behind her father warding off spirits as he wrote his sermons. This, added to the apparent oddness of Emilie herself, convinces Noll that there was a psychotic tendency in the Preiswerks which Carl Jung inherited. Jung's chapter entitled "Confrontation with the Unconscious" in *Memories, Dreams, Reflections* is frequently cited by those who regard his visions and fantasies as psychotic episodes. Henri Ellenberger classes them as "creative illness" (Ellenberger 1970, 447f.).

In my view, Joseph Campbell had the best answer. In a lecture I heard him give, he said that the psychotic and mystic are both immersed in the same water, but the psychotic drowns while the mystic swims. There is little doubt but that Jung was very odd in some ways, and much evidence that he had psychotic episodes on occasion, as well as a history of psychological pathology. At the same time, his ego strength was such that he coped very effectively with his symptoms and was highly productive.

No doubt Jung's inner experiences with his Personality Number Two contributed markedly to his later psychological theories, including the concept of the collective unconscious. They certainly contributed to his concept of complexes in terms of personal psychology. In Jung's mature theory of the human psyche, he sometimes pictured the ego as a fragile archipelago of islands floating in the dark sea of the collective unconscious. The islands are made up of the nuclear ego plus partial egos, so that consciousness is always fragmentary and uncertain. No doubt this concept owed much to his own early psychology and to such experiences as Personality Number Two.

The Quest Deepens

At seventeen, life pushed Jung toward the realities of the work world. At the time, he had no specific plans, a worry for his parents. "The boy is interested in everything imaginable, but he does not know what he wants," Paul Jung complained. Had his son had a prophetic glimpse of the future, he would have known what choice to make. Archaeology. Like Freud, Jung was drawn to it as a teenager and never lost his fascination. The quest for the origins of civilization is intimately related to the inner quest for one's psychological origins. But the University of Basel had no archaeology department. Jung had no money to go elsewhere. He read what he could of Babylonian and Egyptian archaeology at a time when exciting discoveries were just being announced. In turn, that interest was related to his longstanding interest in the history of religions and mythology. One wonders if, at seventeen and eighteen, he had any glimmering of his later theories of myth. Did he see any relationship between myth and dream? He did relate the dreams, visions, and fantasies of his inner world to nature and, by so doing, made his life decision.

During this time, as he wrestled with alternate life choices, Jung had three dreams, two of which occurred at about the same time. In the first he found himself in a dark wood near the Rhine, where he came upon an ancient burial mound. He dug and unearthed fossils. "I must get to know nature," he told himself in the dream, "the world in which we live, and the things around us" (Jung 1961, 85). In the second dream, he was in a wood once again and found himself by a pool, the edges of which were overgrown with foliage. In the pond he saw a giant radiolarian, a marine protozoan with radiating pseudopodia. It seemed beautiful to him, and further convinced him that he must study natural science.

[The dreams] aroused in me an intense desire for knowledge, so that I awoke with a beating heart. These two dreams decided me overwhelmingly in favor of science, and removed all my doubts. (Jung 1961, 85)

The aforementioned dreams did not solve Jung's practical problems, however, which were much the same as those of the young Freud, and were solved the same way. Both wanted to be archeologists; both chose to be research scientists. Both quickly discovered that there were actually only three options to choose among: business, law, or medicine. Both quickly rejected business; Freud dallied briefly with law. Both Freud and Jung soon decided on medicine as the lesser evil, because it was involved with the biological sciences. But neither had the vocation to be a healer.

In Jung's case the problem demanded much dialogue between Personalities Number One and Two:

> Through No. 1's eyes, I saw myself as a rather disagreeable and moderately gifted young man with vaulting ambitions, an undisciplined temperament, and dubious manners, alternating between naive enthusiasm and fits of childish disappointment. (Jung 1961, 86)

Personality Number Two, however, though very vague, expressed a sense of historical continuity, a larger vision. As the two personalities wrestled with one another, Jung had another dream, the third. In this one he found himself struggling against a fierce wind as he made slow headway through the night. In his cupped hands he held a tiny light which he desperately tried to keep lit. He suddenly became aware of something monstrous looming behind him. Looking back, he saw a huge black specter following him. He was terrified. At the same moment, it occurred to him that he must keep the little light glowing despite the wind and the terrors of the night. He realized that the black figure in the swirling mist was his own shadow, and that it had been brought into being by his tiny light. In the dream, he knew that the light was his all-too-fragile consciousness (Jung 1961, 88).

The dream resolved the conflict:

> Now I knew that No. 1 was the bearer of the light, and that No. 2 followed him like a shadow. My task was to shield the light and not look back at the *vita peracta*; this was evidently a forbidden realm of light of a different sort. I must go forward against the storm, which sought to thrust me back into the im-

measurable darkness of a world where one is aware of nothing except the surfaces of things in the background. (Jung 1961, 88)

Jung's worldview swung round, and he saw that his path led out and away from the Eden of childhood and that he must leave Number Two behind. There was something else, besides. Hitherto, he had accepted the conventional wisdom of those days that dreams were from God. Now, in the light of his philosophical reading, he found this answer inadequate and sought another. Why had this insight broken through in a dream? Why a shadow? Was Number Two the creator of dreams?

> He was indeed a specter, a spirit who could hold his own against the world of darkness. This was something I had not known before the dream, and even at the time—I am sure of this in retrospect—I was conscious of it only vaguely, although I knew it emotionally beyond a doubt. (Jung 1961, 89)

During 1892–94, Jung and his father often argued about religion. Carl thought that his father had failed in life, that his golden years had been his student days at Göttingen where he had earned a Ph.D. in Oriental languages.

> He did a great deal of good—far too much—and as a result was usually irritable. Both parents made great efforts to live devout lives, with the result that there were angry scenes between them only too frequently. (Jung 1961, 91)

Carl's personal quest, during these years, was bound up with his ambivalence toward his father. On the one hand, he had keen affection for his father, or so at least he professed in *Memories, Dreams, Reflections.* His affection, however, was much qualified by his painful awareness of his father's inadequacies as a father, or, at least, by what he took to be inadequacies. It is interesting, in this respect, to compare Freud and Jung, both of whom had what they regarded as weak fathers. In later years, both became obsessed with the lack of adequate father figures and tried to put older colleagues in the role. Freud did so with Josef Breuer and Jung with Freud. In both cases, the surrogate fathers also failed.

The European obsession with the father is difficult for most

North Americans to understand, because Canadian and American family patterns (as well as those in Australia and New Zealand) tend to be much more loosely structured and emphasize individualism much more than do those in the rest of the world. In this respect, the American sociologist Theodore Riesmann's tradition-directed, inner-directed, and outer-directed categories are useful.

In Riesmann's terms, Freud, Jung, and virtually all Europeans of the late nineteenth and early twentieth centuries lived in tradition-directed families and communities. The communities were dominated by wise old men, such as the rabbis of eastern European *stetls* and the elders of Swiss villages. Both Jewish and Swiss Protestant families were patriarchal, with clearly defined roles played by mothers, fathers, and children. In both Freud's and Jung's cases, the fathers failed to live up to the expected image. They were not strong and decisive, and their tolerance actually counted against them in the eyes of their sons. Both sons wanted authoritarian role models and did not find them in their fathers.

In Jung's case, role reversal occurred during his father's last years. As his ailing father wasted away, the strong, athletic son carried him about the house in his arms, nurtured him, and also tried to give him the benefit of his religious experience. He pitied his father, but did not respect him. Freud, too, pitied his father, and, being of a people who put exceptional emphasis on "honor thy father and mother," felt deep distress at not being able to do so.

Jung's heated discussions with his father during the latter's final illness, and his associated religious struggles, dominated his thinking during the years between 1892 and 1894. The arguments helped Jung to clarify his own religious position.

Now I understood the deepest meaning of my earlier experience; God Himself had disavowed theology and the Church founded upon it. On the other hand God condoned this theology, as He condoned so much else. It seemed ridiculous to me to suppose that men were responsible for such developments. . . . I was equally sure that none of the theologians I knew had ever seen "the light that shineth in the darkness" with their own eyes, for if they had they would not have been able to teach a "theological religion," which seemed quite inadequate to me, since there was nothing to do with it but believe it without hope. This was what my father had tried valiantly to do, and had run aground. (Jung 1961, 93f.)

What shattered his father's faith (or appeared to) was his reading of psychiatric works, which classed all mental activity as epiphenomena of the brain. Jung regarded that view as "ridiculous materialism."

This, too, was something that one had to believe, just like theology, only in the opposite sense. I felt more certain than ever that both of them lacked epistemological criticism as well as experience. (Jung 1961, 94)

Throughout life, Jung insisted that he was first and foremost an empiricist, but not a materialist. This is abundantly evident in *Memories, Dreams, Reflections.* As a boy, his inquiring mind had turned from observations of nature, to his reading of Biedermann's theological text and Klug's *Philosophical Dictionary*, and finally, to Goethe. All disappointed him because they presented ideas and arguments but not empirical proofs. The same was true of the psychiatry of his day. It consisted of materialistic theories poorly supported by evidence. For that reason, his interest in history led him to the sources, to archaeology, and his interest in science led him to biology. Like Freud, he was oriented toward research, but, in those days, a career in research science was possible only to those with the resources of a Charles Darwin, or the wealth of a Heinrich Schliemann (the discoverer of Troy).

As mentioned, neither Freud nor Jung were interested in patients and healing, just as many scholarly university professors are not so much interested in students as in the subjects they study. They teach to make a living, but would be researchers and writers if they could. Both Freud and Jung ultimately became scholarly scientists after the model provided by the philosophes of the eighteenth-century Enlightenment.

In Basel, Jacob Burckhardt, whom Jung admired from afar, was the kind of scholar he would have liked to have become. Burckhardt, who was independently wealthy, spent his life in highly productive scholarship. In 1903, Jung married wealthy Emma Rauschenbach and followed his example.

It is a well-known fact that many, if not most, psychiatrists and clinical psychologists choose their respective callings because they find people strange and incomprehensible. This was true of Freud and Jung. Both were somewhat alienated from their fellows, Jung especially, and both found human motivation at first difficult to understand.

Thus, as in Freud's case, Jung finally decided on medicine for a variety of reasons, none of which included a passionate desire to heal the sick. In those days, few physicians became wealthy, but most made a decent living.

With the help of a working scholarship, a loan from an uncle, and the help of other family members, Jung was able to enroll at Basel University in a day when few Europeans (or Americans, for that matter) were privileged to do so. He began his studies during the spring of 1895.

Four

God Defecates on Basel Cathedral

Jung's Philosophical Development

Jung underwent a religious crisis in 1887 when he was around thirteen:

> One fine summer day . . . I came out of school at noon and went to the cathedral square. The sky was gloriously blue, the day one of radiant sunshine. The roof of the cathedral glittered, the sun sparkling from the new, brightly glazed tiles. I was overwhelmed by the beauty of the sight, and thought: "The world is beautiful and the church is beautiful, and God made all this and sits above it far away in the blue sky on a golden throne and . . ." (Jung 1961, 36)

At that point, a further thought almost came to him unbidden—a blasphemous thought which filled him with dread. "Don't go on thinking now!" he told himself. But the image of the cathedral kept imposing itself on him. Something terrible was coming. It occurred to him that this compulsive thought was a sin against the Holy Ghost, the one kind of sin for which there was no divine pardon. Anyone who commits that sin is damned to hell for all eternity, he thought. The thought obsessed him all the way home and he arrived much upset (Jung 1961, 36).

He tossed restlessly that night, unable to sleep, and was profoundly disturbed the next day and the day after that. His parents were alarmed and bewildered. Then it occurred to Carl that he was descended from Adam and Eve, who had no parents but were created directly by God, who had intentionally made them as they were. They were compelled to be what God wanted them to be. "They were perfect creatures of God, for he creates only perfection, and yet they committed the first sin by doing what God did not want them to do. How was that possible?" (Jung 1961, 38). One wonders if a thirteen-year-old boy could have such notions; theologically, this is Infralapsarianism, a thorny, controversial issue at the Synod of Dort in 1607. However, Jung recalled that the more he thought about Adam and Eve the more convinced he became that God willed Adam and Eve to sin. Instantly, he felt liberated, as in the classical Protestant conversion experience. God himself had put these defiant thoughts in his mind!

> I gathered all my courage, as though I were about to leap forthwith into hell-fire, and let the thought come. I saw before me the cathedral, the blue sky. God sits on His golden throne, high above the world—and from under the throne an enormous turd falls upon the sparkling new roof, shatters it, and breaks the walls of the cathedral asunder.
>
> So that was it! I felt an enormous, an indescribable relief. Instead of the expected damnation, grace had come upon me, and with it an unutterable bliss such as I had never known. I wept for happiness and gratitude. The wisdom and goodness of God had been revealed to me now that I had yielded to His inexorable command. It was as though I had experienced an illumination. A great many things I had not previously understood became clear to me. (Jung 1961, 39b)

The boy thought to himself: God had made Adam and Eve to think what they did not want to think and thus to do what they did not want to do. He had made all his creatures that way. To obey God in all things is to obey whatever one thinks. "One must be utterly abandoned to God," he told himself, "nothing matters but fulfilling His will. Otherwise, all is folly and meaninglessness."

> Why did God befoul His cathedral? That, for me, was a terrible thought. But then came the dim understanding that God could be something terrible. I had experienced a dark and terrible secret. It overshadowed my whole life, and I became deeply pensive. (Jung 1961, 40)

Years later, Jung realized that the experience was his rejection of conventional piety symbolized by the cathedral, the communion service which so repelled him, his father's doctrinal sermons, and the grim piety of his parishioners.

The boy had had a prophetic vision of divine glory contrasted with the conventional secular religion and of a church that had lost its soul. Marie-Louise von Franz suggests that even as a boy, Jung was somehow aware of Nietzsche's madman, who goes out in the marketplace shouting "God is dead!" But Nietzsche, who indeed did impress Jung later, during his university student years, had very little impact until the late 1890s. Perhaps Jung imbibed the spiritual crisis of the materialistic nineteenth century by osmosis.

Less remarkably, the boy was entranced by the thought of God in nature and as the creator of nature. This is a common sentiment among young people of rustic origins. In *Memories, Dreams, Reflections*, the octogenarian Jung presents a version of his religious experience that is far too advanced and subtle for any lad of thirteen.

> For nature seemed, like myself, to have been set aside by God as non-divine, although created by Him as an expression of Himself. Nothing could persuade me that "in the image of God" applied only to man. In fact it seemed to me that the high mountains, the rivers, lakes, trees, flowers, and animals far better exemplified the essence of God than men with their ridiculous clothes, their meanness, vanity, mendacity, and abhorrent egotism. (Jung 1961, 45)

This is where God was, not in the church.

It is not at all strange that Jung's first communion was a disappointment. His godfather, a grave, elderly wheelwright, came for him clad in frock coat and top hat. It was a very solemn occasion. They walked to the church together in silence. At the service the boy ate a piece of stale bread and took a swallow of sour wine. The boy knew the tavern where the wine came from. The men were stiff, solemn, and bored. "I saw no sadness and no joy, and felt that the feast was meager in every respect," he wrote in his autobiography. It was all so perfunctory. Later he walked home with his father. Carl was wearing a black felt hat and a jacket which had been lengthened. In his imagination, his felt hat turned into a top hat and his jacket into a frock coat. He felt that he was turning into a peasant in Sunday best. His first communion was supposed to have been a religious initiation, but it was only a very stuffy ritual that had nothing to do with the real God, whom Carl had experienced in fantasy and in compulsive, unbidden thoughts in his mind. The so-called Christian religion had nothing to do with God. "On the other hand," he mused, "it was quite clear that Jesus, the man, did have to do with God; he had despaired in Gethsemane and on the cross, after having taught that God was a kind and loving father. He too, then, must have seen the fearfulness of God." The boy became convinced that communion was a travesty; to him, a meaningless ritual. "'Why, that is not religion at all,' I thought. 'It is an absence of God; the church is a place I should not go to. It is not life which is there, but death'" (Jung 1961, 55).

No wonder God defecated on Basel Cathedral in Jung's fantasy! It is also no wonder that Jung had his own very secret religion from an early age. His relationship to the church shattered at this moment. His awareness of God deepened. It occurred to him that conventional Christianity, like the Münster, is manmade, and this is why the celestial deity of his fantasy had defecated on it.

> God is not human, I thought; that is His greatness, that nothing human impinges on Him. He is kind and terrible—both at once—and is therefore a great peril from which everyone naturally tries to save himself. People cling one-sidedly to His love and goodness, for fear they will fall victim to the tempter and destroyer. Jesus, too, had noticed that, and had therefore taught: "Lead us not into temptation." (Jung 1961, 55)

The boy decided that he had not invented that strange image of God defecating on the cathedral, nor the dream of the underground phallus.

> A stronger will than mine had imposed both on me. Had nature been responsible? But nature was nothing other than the will of the Creator. Nor did it help to accuse the devil, for he too was a creature of God. God alone was real—an annihilating fire and an indescribable grace. (Jung 1961, 55)

Memories, Dreams, Reflections may tell us much more about the octogenarian Jung than of the schoolboy. One can make too much of childhood and pubertal religious experiences. They are very commonplace. Many children undergo religious crises at the onset of adolescence. It is a time when many children discover their own identity. About that time, they also become aware of the reality of their own mortality. Some react against conventional religion as Jung did: others experience conversion.

Strange to say, Jung in his mature years ignored child psychology, despite the vividness of his own childhood experiences and their importance to him. Very little of his clinical work was with children, and, according to his wife, he virtually ignored his own children when they were young. On one occasion, during the early 1930s, he conducted a seminar on child psychology, but it was based entirely on the reminiscences of adults. Jung often said that the inner world of childhood should not be intruded upon by adults. As a matter of principle, he refused to analyze children's dreams and fantasies, and did not consider the inner life of childhood to be important. How strange, when he devoted so much time to exploring his own childhood memories!

In his memoirs, Jung tells us that when he reached adolescence, Personality Number One came to the fore and Personality Number Two faded, not to reappear until the crisis after his break with Freud. During these youthful years, Jung, like most young men, devoted himself to his education and to career building. He also read very widely, so much so that his father worried what would become of him, because he was interested in everything except a practical way to earn a living.

Like many thoughtful young people, Carl was perplexed by the problem of evil and the inconsistency between a God of Love and suffering. Jung's God was not the "good" God of his father's sermon, but a subtle Being in which good and evil were one. One doubts, however, that a thirteen-year-old had so many weighty theological problems on his mind.

Jung's mother suggested that he read Goethe's *Faust*, and he did. "It poured into my soul like a miraculous balm." However, the boy had the impression that the weight of the drama lay on the side of Mephistopheles. Faust was a pompous windbag, a fool. He deserved damnation, not last-minute reprieve and initiation into God's mysteries. Although Carl was impressed with Goethe, he was disappointed. Goethe seemed to be a prophet who showed no way out of the problem he was wrestling with.

Goethe, however, had introduced Carl to philosophy. As a teenager, Jung read Schopenhauer, who at first seemed to have the answer to the problem of evil. But Carl was unconvinced by the theory of blind, world-creating will. To him, it seemed a poor explanation. When he was around seventeen, he read Kant's *Critique of Pure Reason*. Kant impressed him much more, and he was still reading Kant when he went to university and was well into his medical studies. Jung was especially drawn to the idea of the *a priori*. He also read Eduard von Hartmann's *Philosophy of the Unconscious*, Paul Carus's *Psyche*, F. W. Schelling, and other German nature philosophers. From Ernst Haeckel, he derived the idea that ontogeny recapitulates phylogeny. The individual passes through the same evolutionary stages as the species.

Von Hartmann invented the term *Unconscious* (*Das Unbewusste*), and it was from him, as well as from Kant, Schopenhauer, Carus, and Nietzsche, that Jung learned about the concept of hidden mind. The idea of universal psyche dawned on him as a philosophical principle, and he may have connected it with the intuitions, dreams, and visions of his childhood.

Leibbrand (1954) thinks that most of Jung's philosophical ideas can be traced to Schelling, but Jung scarcely makes mention of him. Most scholars think that Jung was primarily influenced by Kant. In later years, Jung often mentioned von Hartmann and Carus. Noll, as we have seen, traces his concepts to *Völkisch* thinkers as well as to Haeckel, Blavatsky, the nature philosophers, and Nietzsche.

There was keen interest in parapsychology and the occult at the turn of the century, and Jung shared it to an extraordinary degree. He came by it naturally because of his maternal grandfather, Samuel Preiswerk, who used to hold weekly conversations with the spirit of his first wife—to the intense annoyance of his second wife. Jung's mother was psychic and sometimes made enigmatic statements, as though from another personality. During Carl's university years, strange episodes occurred, as when a sturdy old table suddenly cracked and a bread knife snapped into several pieces. Such experiences went far to convince him that reality had deeper dimensions than the visible world.

At the beginning of his paper "Archetypes of the Collective Unconscious," Jung stated that he derived the idea of the unconscious from reading the works of Carus and von Hartmann. As Jung points out, the idea of the unconscious "had gone down under the overwhelming wave of materialism and empiricism, leaving hardly a ripple behind it, it gradually reappeared in the scientific domain of medical psychology" (Jung 1954a, par. 1).

In "Conscious, Unconscious, and Individuation," he refers to the nature philosophers again. "The philosophers Carus and von Hartmann treat the unconscious as a metaphysical principle, a sort of universal mind, without any trace of personality or ego-consciousness, and similarly Schopenhauer's 'Will' is without an ego." Jung adds that "modern psychologists, too, regard the unconscious as an egoless function below the threshold of consciousness. Unlike the philosophers, they tend to derive its subliminal functions from the conscious mind" (Jung 1939, 492, 276f.).

Jung's indebtness to Kant has been frequently noted, and acknowledged by Jung himself. In "Psychological Aspects of the Mother Archetype" he observed, based on Kant:

There *is* an *a priori* factor in all human activities, namely the inborn, preconscious and unconscious individual structure of the psyche. (Jung 1954c, 77)

Elsewhere in the same essay he adds that the archetypes are among the inalienable assets of every psyche. They form the "treasure in the realm of shadowy thoughts" of which Kant spoke, and of which we have ample evidence in the countless treasure motifs of mythology.

As mentioned, Jung read the nature philosophers, Schopenhauer, Nietzsche, and Kant during his gymnasium years, and continued to read them on weekends and during holidays after he entered the University of Basel as a medical student. He was also fascinated by prehistoric, Babylonian, and Egyptian archaeology, fields in which exciting new discoveries were being made; what was then called comparative religions was very much in its infancy.

Whether it is from an American high school today or a Swiss-German gymnasium during the nineteenth century, finishing secondary school is a rite of passage. It is childhood's end. Jung realized, as do all teenagers, the significance of the step. Indeed it is the most drastic transition a person makes in life. Until around age eighteen, most middle-class people live in the bosom of a family, usually under parental care. It is appropriate for the child to play, just as young animals do, play being practice for life. It is not usually appropriate to work, nor to bear much responsibility. At eighteen the priorities reverse.

For young, middle-class Swiss of the late nineteenth century, the rite of passage of maturity meant either entering one's life's work or entering some kind of vocational apprenticeship such as university. University is not like secondary school; it is career-related for most. Maturity also means courtship. Few young Europeans courted before eighteen in those days. In Switzerland, coming of age also meant compulsory military training in the citizen army. All of these were maturation experiences designed to force the boy to become a man. Women, of course, had their own equivalents, preparations for marriage and motherhood.

Jung's transition from boy to man was delayed. He stayed home until 1900 when, at age twenty-four, he finished medical school and set off for Zürich and a new life. University is *in loco parentis*, a sort of midpassage from childhood to maturity, and the student does not make the break from family home to personal independence abruptly but gradually. This was so in Jung's case.

The years 1895 through 1900 were therefore years of transition for Jung. But during this five-year period of medical school, Jung took on the responsibilities of being head of the household in his father's stead, and also became much more socialized than he had been. At the same time, he retained much of his boyhood imaginal qualities, his childlike love of nature, his preoccupation with fantasy and dreams, and his equally childlike spirituality. He was never to lose touch with the inner child, but continued to regress in service of the ego. That capacity, in my view, accounts for his lifelong quest for enlightenment.

Five

Barrel

A Young Fox

During the spring of 1895, Carl enrolled as a medical student at the University of Basel and became a "young fox," as first-year students were called. A year later, he joined Zofingia, the student fraternity, and was given another nickname, *Walze* or "Barrel," "Steam Roller," perhaps because of his stocky build, or perhaps because of his inordinate capacity for beer—or both. From the start he was a good student, happily liberated from gymnasium, which he had hated, and pleased to study biology and to learn the scientific method. He was a good science student, but was soon put off by the mechanistic materialism of most of his professors and fellow students. To him, this was just one more form of orthodoxy and it repelled him as much as theology had. Money was a problem, but his father managed part of it and was able to raise the rest.

The 1890s were hard times for the Jung family. Paul Jung was stricken with his terminal illness the year Carl enrolled. It was never diagnosed, but was probably cancer.

In January 1896, Carl came home from lectures. He asked his mother how his father was. His mother told him that he was very weak. Then his father whispered something to his mother which Carl did not understand: he asked if Carl had passed the state examinations. That would complete his medical studies for the Matura, after which he would have to do a dissertation followed by an oral defense of his thesis. On completion of that, he would be awarded his doctorate in medicine. The state examinations were therefore an important step in higher education in countries of German-speaking Europe.

Carl, of course, had just begun university, and was in his first year of medical school. His mother signaled with her eyes that he must lie, and so he told his father that he had indeed passed his exams and therefore earned the Matura. His father sighed with relief. His mother went into the next room and left Carl alone with his father. He heard a rattling in his father's throat, the death rattle. "I stood by his bed, fascinated," Jung wrote in *Memories, Dreams, Reflections*, "I had never seen anyone die before." His father suddenly stopped breathing, and Carl went to his mother who was knitting in the next room. "He is dying," he told her. They went to the father's room together. He was dead. "How quickly it has all passed," his mother said (Jung 1961, 95f.).

Some readers of *Memories* accuse Jung of callousness, but he adds that the next days were sorrowful and dismal. Many people, perhaps most, are awed by the presence of death; fascinated, in fact. Grief often comes later. In other words, what Jung writes of his father's death and his own reaction at the time does not seem very remarkable, especially when death follows a prolonged illness and has been long expected. What struck Jung more was a chance remark his mother made in what Jung calls her Number Two voice. She said, "He died in time for you." At the time, it seemed to mean that his father's death had removed a burden, and that Jung could get on with his life and career. However, the words "for you" deeply affected him. It was childhood's end. Now he must assume manly responsibilities but now, too, he was free.

He moved into his father's room soon after the funeral, and also took his father's place as head of the family. His father had managed the household finances badly, and his mother could not manage money at all. There were many things to be done. They had to vacate the parsonage, leave Klein-Hüningen, and find quarters elsewhere. They moved to a run-down Alsatian cottage at Bottminger Mill beyond the Nightingale Woods, still within walking distance of Basel.

Among Europeans of that day the death of a father automatically made the eldest son head of the household, a responsibility keenly felt. It meant that the son took on the father's patriarchal role and was expected to support the family, to manage household finance, to make family decisions, and to behave in an authoritative way. His mother and siblings were expected to obey him as they had his father; to defer to him as the person who sat at the head of the dining room table, to accept his guidance, and to obey his commands. It was a heavy burden for a twenty-one year old; it also encouraged self-importance.

Jung's father appeared to Carl in a dream six weeks after his death. People frequently dream about the deceased after there has been a death in the family. In the dream, his father stood before him and told him that he had been on holiday and was coming home; that he had made a good recovery. Also in the dream, Jung was anxious lest his father think that he had been impertinent in moving into his father's room, but his father was not in the least annoyed. This was a recurrent dream. Jung had it again not long after. It made him wonder if such dreams had hidden meaning, and also caused him to think about life after death for the first time (Jung 1961, 96f.).

Paul Jung's death left the family destitute in an era when widows and orphans languished in Dickensian-style poverty all over the world. As in *Nicholas Nickleby*, a bereaved widow and her children were left to the dubious charity of their better-situated relatives. The Preiswerks fitted this category. They were among the leading families of Basel, and most of them enjoyed affluence and status. They were highly respectable and had a high opinion of themselves as Swiss clerical counterparts of Galsworthy's Forsytes.

Carl's maternal uncles had been condescending to Jung's parents when his father was alive, and regarded them as poor relations. Now they were disdainful of Carl. Several uncles thought that Carl should withdraw from university and take a job as a clerk. He, however, was determined to continue his education somehow, as well as provide for his mother and sister. He went to the uncle he trusted most, hoping for some financial help as well as advice. "His uncle just looked at him, however, took his pipe out of his mouth, and said: 'Well, that is how one learns to be a man, my boy.'" Jung was furious and stalked out. However, before he reached home, he had thought it over and realized that his uncle was right; that he did have to fend for himself. "Why, that is the best advice he could possibly have given," he told himself (Hannah 1976, 64).

Carl now realized that he was head of the household; that he had to be the provider. He also realized that since his mother was utterly inept at handling money, he would have to manage the domestic finances as well.

Inconsistently, he did accept some financial help from the youngest of his maternal uncles. Another uncle, on his father's side, lent him enough money to stay in university, and, when he finished his studies, Jung owed him a thousand francs. Jung provided the rest of the family income and the remainder of his tuition from a job as junior assistant at the university and from the commission he earned from an aunt for selling a large collection of antiques. He also took over the practice of a Dr. Heinrich Pestalozzi during the latter's summer vacations.

Dr. Pestalozzi was located in the village of Männedorf on Lake Zürich. According to Barbara Hannah, Jung enjoyed the experience. For one thing, it may have been his first visit to Lake Zürich. Dr. Pestalozzi had a country practice and, as these were the days of house calls, it meant much walking through the countryside to scattered farms and cottages. Jung enjoyed the walks, and also felt at ease with the patients, most of whom were peasants, the kind of people among which he had grown up. Although he often felt inadequate to the demands of the practice because of inexperience, it caused him to think that he might like to be a country doctor (Hannah 1976, 65).

These were busy days. Jung did well in medical school, and became first a junior assistant in anatomy and then a demonstrator in charge of the course in histology. The latter was a junior research position. He enjoyed most of his courses, worked hard, and earned the high regard of most of his professors. He had high marks in histology and anatomy, and set his sights on internal medicine as his specialization.

He hated physiology because of vivisection, which he vigorously objected to because of the barbarous treatment of animals. He considered most of it unnecessary. He had, as he told Barbara Hannah, an unconscious identity with animals. Because of his antipathy to vivisection he barely scraped through the physiology course.

He also disliked psychiatry. F. Wille, the professor of psychiatry at Basel University, had a physiological orientation which, to Jung, was not very interesting, and he found the course boring. The elderly psychiatrist supervised the Basel mental hospital, and had a purely custodial approach. In those days, psychiatry was based on the theory that psychosis was caused by the physical degeneration of the brain.

Despite the rigors of medical school, Jung made time for religious studies. He often talked with an erudite friend of his father's, a theologian who introduced him to the theology of Albrecht Ritschl (1822–1889), which was very much in vogue among European Protestants during the 1890s. Like Ernst Troeltsch and Adolf Harnack, Ritschl emphasized the ethical teachings of the historical Jesus and the social teachings of the Christian Church. As when he was a boy, Jung was repelled by Christocentrism. At the same time, he was equally repelled by the modernist theology of so many of the theological students. Jung therefore found himself caught between orthodoxy, which he had rejected, and liberalism, which seemed to be lacking in spirituality. The discussions convinced him that "in religious matters only experience counted" (Jung 1961, 98).

On Sundays, instead of going to church, Jung stayed in his room studying philosophy, especially Kant, von Hartmann, and Schopenhauer. After some hesitation, he also read Nietzsche.

Nietzsche had taught at Basel during his youth. He was then a brilliant young man and, indeed, had been appointed to a chair in philosophy when he was twenty-four. During the 1890s, he was still remembered by some in Basel, usually with derision. Jung was perplexed by him and also disturbed that he might be like him and suffer the same fate (Jung 1961, 98).

Nevertheless, Jung was in awe of Nietzsche who, like him, had been a minister's son. However, the latter "had been born in the great land of Germany," spoke High German, and knew Latin and Greek as well as several modern languages besides his own. Compared to him, Jung felt like an ignorant country bumpkin. Nietzsche was very special, and could afford to ignore what people thought of him, but Carl did not feel free to be an eccentric himself. ". . . I must not let myself find out how far I might be like him" (Jung 1961, 102).

Zarathustra struck a sympathetic chord in Jung. It was the voice of another's Number Two Personality, discovered late in life when Nietzsche was already past middle age. Jung had known his own Number Two Personality since he was thirteen, and had learned to be cautious, to live in the closet.

Nietzsche "came out," gave his Number Two the name *Ar-rheton*, and talked about him openly.

Unflattering gossip about Nietzsche and his *Arrheton* still circulated, stories of how he used to put on airs as a gentleman, and his stylistic exaggerations. Idiosyncrasy and eccentricity were not tolerated in staid Basel, and Nietzsche had suffered for it. He had naively hoped to find people who would share his visions and grasp his "transvaluation of all values," but never had. He had been disappointed. He found himself surrounded by philistines, and had been foolish enough to scatter his pearls before swine. They had ridiculed him and, in reaction, he had become bombastic in language, piling up metaphors that were constantly misunderstood. The world had been deaf to him, "And he fell—tightrope-walker that he proclaimed himself to be—into depths far beyond himself" (Jung 1961, 103).

Jung was afraid that he would suffer the same fate if he revealed his innermost thoughts and experiences. Consequently, his fellow students had little awareness of Jung's Personality Number Two.

Albert Oeri and Gustav Steiner, two former classmates, later recalled the Jung they knew (Personality Number One): a very brash, outspoken young man, very sure of himself, domineering and not at all reluctant to pose in public. He was sometimes rather aggressive and egotistical, a glib talker who entranced them with his chatter, anything but retiring or withdrawn. He was opinionated and conceited. He was also very sociable and usually good natured—apparently an extravert. In 1965, Steiner read Jung's chapter entitled "Student Years" with astonishment. It was not a Jung he had ever met.

We have rare glimpses of Jung the university student in the entries in his diary that were published by Aniela Jaffé in *C. G. Jung: Word and Image*. Jung wrote the four entries during November and December 1898.

November 1898:

[Scholars?] . . . are cold and merciless and with curious fingers poke around in the incurable wound of those great ones, which has begun to bleed again. How is it possible to remain objective in the face of human helplessness? As if they were not human beings; as if they had no heart, as if they were history itself, or a history-writing robot! Poor people, deprived of their hearts, slaves to the lifeless idol of science.

November 1898:

The sight of the cloudy sky has a titanic quality. The towering masses of clouds seem to want to crush the cowering earth. They heave along at an incredible altitude.[sic] gigantic peaks dipped in glowing sunlight, great abysses flooded with light, and stretching above it all in infinite clarity and stillness the blue sky. —And the meteorologist photographs this simple little phenomenon: caption: cumuli, that is, "heaped clouds."

November 1898:

The cosmic bodies are the tears which the universe wept at Lucifer's fall.

December 1898:

My situation is mirrored in my dreams. Often glorious, portentous glimpses of flowery landscapes, infinite blue seas, sunny coasts, but often, too, images of unknown roads shrouded in night, of friends who take leave of me to stride toward a brighter fate, of myself alone on barren paths facing impenetrable darkness. "Oh, fling yourself into a positive faith," my grandfather Jung writes. Yes, I would be glad to fling myself if I could, if that depended only on the uppermost me. But an inexplicable heavy something, a listnesses and numbness, weariness and weakness, always prevents the decisive final step. I have already taken many steps, but I am still a long way from the final one. The greater the certainty, the more superhuman the doubts, the destructive hellish powers. (Jaffé 1979, 27)

Here we have a Jung who is naive, sensitive, and reflective, very much as he was as a boy. His romantic love of nature has continued, as has his skepticism concerning science and his loathing of the materialism of the age. Jung loved nature and hated the dehumanized aspects of a Europe in the throes of the industrial revolution. It is the Jung whom we readily recognize as the boy who was the father of the old Jung who wrote *Memories, Dreams, Reflections* in his eighties.

The Jung whom his friends knew was their Zofingian fraternity brother. Jung joined in May 1896. Like many of the German *Burschenschaften*, Zofingia was founded just after the
Napoleonic Wars by young liberals who shared the Pan-
German idealism of their German counterparts. Later, Swiss
nationalism prevailed, but otherwise the Zofingians were like
other German university fraternity brothers. They wore military uniforms, partied a great deal, and drank a lot of beer.
They also had weekly sessions at which provocative lectures
were given on controversial topics followed by lively arguments. Jung became a participant during his second semester
and gave five lectures, which have been recently published.
They are his earliest published works.

"Barrel" was fun-loving and convivial. His friend Albert
Oeri remembered him as a "very merry" Zofingian. He and his
friends drank at the Breo, the tavern in the Steinen district
where bibulous Zofingians gathered, went to parties and
dances, and joined in the usual boisterous fun.

Before the family moved, Jung spent Sundays in his father's
old room where he studied Kant, Schopenhauer, and von Hartmann rather than go to church. He also wrote entries in his
diary, confiding to it his romantic love of nature, as well as his
ruminations and monologues about the psyche. Unfortu-
nately, these have not yet been made available to scholars.

In his quiet moods, Jung was hidden, discreet, sensitive,
spiritual, and psychic. He experienced God every day in the
natural world and in the deepest impulses and emotions of his
being. He also trafficked with spirits. Everyone knew Barrel,
but no one knew the Jung with strange fantasies, dreams, and
mysteries. He still pondered the dream of the underground
phallus king, but had forgotten the manikin in the pencil box.
He was still perplexed by his vision of God defecating on Basel
cathedral, and his more recent dream of the shadow, in which
he tried to keep alight a small lamp. He was very secretive
about these matters. He experienced illuminations and inner
revelations of the numinous, but he spoke of them to no one.

Barrel had nothing to do with any of that. He was too busy
with his medical studies, laboratory work, and family responsibilities. But according to Oeri, he also had a juvenile love af-
fair. It happened during a festival at the town of Zofingen, for

which the fraternity was named. Jung had never been fond of dancing, but actually danced quite well, and especially on this particular occasion. He fell madly in love with a girl from French Switzerland and impulsively decided to propose marriage to her. Soon after, he went to a jeweler and placed twenty centimes on the counter for an engagement ring. It was not nearly enough and when the jeweler told him so, Jung flew into a rage and stormed out of the shop cursing the shopkeeper for ruining his love life. As far as Oeri knew, it was Jung's one such venture during his student days (Oeri 1970, 186).

As when he was a boy, Barrel was mischievous, always in the mood for pranks, the companion of youthful escapades. One has this impression of him from photographs from his student days. He is a good fellow among his uniformed, booted fellow Zofingians, reminding one of Shriners on a spree. One has the impression that, contrary to his comments in his memoirs, he was popular.

The "Wise Old Man" of the eighteenth century eventually surfaced during Jung's confrontation with the unconscious between 1913 and 1918. He became Elijah, and also the winged, horned old man whom he called Philemon. Another personality also appeared. She was Salome, the blind girl who accompanied Elijah. She was his anima, the feminine component of his psyche. There is no hint of her in Jung's early life, but she must have been there. Quite clearly, however, Jung's bewigged gentleman of the eighteenth century, who rode in a fine carriage, was the earliest personification of the Wise Old Man whom Jung later knew as Philemon. Jung was inwardly attuned to the deep mystery that he was to later identify as the collective unconscious.

From his reading of Schopenhauer, von Hartmann, Kant, and Carl Gustav Carus, Jung knew the *idea* of the unconscious as a university student. He had experienced the hidden dimensions of mind in childhood visions, fantasies, and dreams. But, as yet, he had not drawn the connection between Kant's theory of the noumena and his own early experiences. That was to come years later, in 1909, when a dream aboard ship revealed the collective unconscious to him. That dream, in turn, inspired him to study myth, and by so doing, to discover the mythic nature of psychotic hallucinations.

Barrel Discovers the Occult

At the end of his second semester at university, Jung found a small book of psychic phenomena in the library of a classmate's father, an art historian. The book was around twenty years old and had been written by a theologian. Jung was fascinated. As a country boy, he had grown up on tales about supernatural occurrences since his earliest years, and he readily believed that the stories were true. If so, why did such events happen all over the world? He did not think it was because of religion, because there were so many different religions throughout the world. "Rather it must be connected with the objective behavior of the human psyche. . . . I could find out absolutely nothing, except what the philosophers said" (Jung 1961, 99).

Jung's factual knowledge was being extended by his courses in science and natural philosophy. Science and the scientific method impressed him deeply. He was particularly affected by the precision and accuracy of it, by experimental verification. However, he was also impressed by its limits, the point he was to make in his first Zofingia address. Scientific research, even then, was very specialized and reductionist. From Jung's point of view, too many scientists suffered from a lack of imagination and, what was worse, a resistance to new ideas. Jung also felt a lack of depth and comprehensiveness. Scientific knowledge was too fragmented. It lacked the larger perspectives that drew him to philosophy, and especially to Kant and Schopenhauer. Jung was convinced of Kant's *Ding an sich* (thing in itself) theory of God, also, that the psyche lay behind all physical phenomenon. He was deeply influenced by the discredited vitalists, and especially von Hartmann, whose theories of the unconscious were essentially derived from Schopenhauer. Von Hartmann had been the most widely read and discussed philosopher of the sixties and seventies, but during the late eighties and nineties he was all but forgotten. There had been a shift in intellectual mood from vitalism, holism, and idealism to mechanistic materialism, specialization, and realism.

Jung read Johann K. Zollner's *Transcendental Physics and So-Called Philosophy* (1879) and books on psychic phenomena by the English chemist William Crookes as well as Kant's *Dreams of the Spirit Seer* and the writings of Karl Duprel

(1839–99), who advanced a "monistic doctrine of the soul." He read older works as well: Eschenmayer and Joseph Gorres, for instance, who were of the circle to which the Swiss-born Anton Mesmer belonged. He read the works of the French theosophist Louis-Claude de Sainte Martin, Friedrich Oberlin, Heinrich Jung-Stilling, and all seven volumes of Emanuel Swedenborg as well as the works of the Frankfort physician Johann Carl Passavant (1790–1857) and Justinus Kerner's *The Seeress of Prevorst* (1829). He read, he tells us, virtually the whole of the literature of parapsychology available to him at the time, especially that in German.

He constantly talked about psychic phenomena with his friends at university. In *Memories, Dreams, Reflections*, he says that most were skeptical and derisive. However, they thought enough of his Zofingia talks to publish them, and enough of him to elect him president of the fraternity. Jung was particularly fascinated with how defensive some of his friends were when the subject came up, and that more than a few seemed anxious. He was already looking for hidden psychological motives.

According to Oeri, Barrel was always prepared to revolt against the "League of Virtue," as he called the organized fraternity brothers, meaning, one presumes, that he was something of a rebel.

> Once, when we couldn't get a speaker, Jung suggested that we might hold a discussion without specifying the topic. The minutes read, "Jung *vulgo* 'Barrel', the pure spirit having gone to his head, urged that we debate hitherto unresolved philosophical questions. This was agreeable to all, more agreeable than might have been expected under our usual 'prevailing circumstances.' But 'Barrel' blithered endlessly, and that was dumb. Oeri, *vulgo* 'It,' likewise spiritually oiled, distorted, in so far as such was still possible, these barreling thoughts . . ." At the next meeting, Jung succeeded in having the word "blithered," which he held to be too subjective, struck from the minutes and substituted by the word "talked." (Oeri 1970, 186f.)

According to Oeri, Jung usually dominated the fifty or sixty students from various faculties of the university, "luring them into highly speculative areas of thought, which to the majority of us were an alien wonderland. When he gave his paper

'Einige Gedanken über Psychologie' ('Some Thoughts on Psychology'), as club secretary I could have recorded some thirty discussion topics" (Oeri 1970, 187).

As Oeri said, materialism dominated the academic world during the last decades of the nineteenth century, especially among scientists and physicians, but also among scholars in the humanities. "Yet despite this, Jung, by choice an outsider, was able to keep everyone under his intellectual thumb." Oeri confirms Jung's keen interest in the esoteric and occult during these years:

> This was possible—and I would not wish to conceal it—because he had courageously schooled himself, intensively studying occult literature, conducting parapsychological experiments, and finally standing by the convictions he derived therefrom, except where corrected by the result of more careful and detailed psychological studies. (Oeri 1970, 187)

Jung's mother shared her son's enthusiasm for the occult, but his university friends did not. "I had the feeling," Jung said, "that I had pushed to the brink of the world; what was of burning interest to me was null and void for others, and even a cause for dread" (Jung 1961, 100).

Oeri confirms Jung's lament that his interest in psychic phenomena was often greeted with skepticism.

> He was appalled that the official scientific position of the day toward occult phenomena was simply to deny their existence, rather than to investigate and explain them. For this reason, spiritualists such as Zöllner and Crookes, about whose teachings he could speak for hours, became for him heroic martyrs of science.

However,

> Among his friends and relatives he found participants for séances. I cannot say anything more detailed about them, for I was at the time so deeply involved in Kantian critique that I could not be drawn in myself. My psychic opposition would have neutralized the atmosphere. (Oeri 1970, 187)

Jung loved to lecture his friends, according to Oeri. While lecturing, Oeri wrote,

His dear little dachshund would look at me so earnestly, just as though he understood every word, and Jung did not fail to tell me how the sensitive animal would sometimes whimper pitiously when occult forces were active in the house. (Oeri 1970, 187f.)

One guesses that Jung did not so much offend his friends with his incredible theories as bore them. From student photographs of him, stocky, intense, and uniformed like a soldier, one has the impression that he could be overbearing at times.

Sometimes he would sit late into the night with his drinking buddies at the Breo:

Afterwards, he didn't like walking home alone through the sinister Nightingale Woods all the way to the Bottminger Mill [to which he, his mother and sister moved after his father's death in 1896]. As we were leaving the tavern, therefore, he would simply begin talking to one of us of something especially interesting, and so one would accompany him, without noticing it, right to his front door. Along the way he might interrupt himself by noting, "On this spot Doctor Götz was murdered," or something like that. In parting, he would offer his revolver for the trip back. I was not afraid of Dr. Götz's ghost, nor of living evil spirits, but I was afraid of Jung's revolver in my pocket. (Oeri 1970, 188)

To Jung, the lack of enthusiasm for Spiritualism and the occult on the part of his fellow students was partly because the subject frightened them. The topic seemed to make his friends uneasy. Jung, who may have failed to notice yawns and glazed eyes when he got on to his favorite topic, put their resistance down to anxiety. That fascinated him, because it proved his case. Perhaps the skeptics actually were subconsciously aware of the esoteric, but repressed their awareness. Years later Jung said the same of Freud and his atheism, observing how agitated Freud became during their meeting in Vienna in 1910 at which Freud excitedly warned Jung against the "black mud of the occult." To Jung, Freud seemed to have repressed the occult and religion the way others did their sexuality. Indeed, his sexual theories seemed to be a defense against the occult.

Jung was perplexed by the vehemence of the unbelievers; by their intensity. What were they afraid of? He thought that their attitude was highly unscientific because they would not listen to the evidence and refused to hear it. Their minds were closed, as much so as the orthodox Christians who refused to consider the case for biological evolution. They ridiculed the learned professors of Bologna who refused to look through Galileo's telescope, but they would listen to no ideas that clashed with their materialism. Jung was appalled by the inconsistency.

He, too, had his reservations about parapsychology, esotericism, and the occult, just as he had his doubts about religion. However, he was willing to consider the evidence. He insisted that anyone who considered himself to be a scientist or scholar must consider all possibilities. He did not regard science as a body of proven data, as so many of his fellow students seemed to, but as hypotheses constantly subject to revision on the basis of testing. In that way, Jung was much more dedicated to scientific principle than were most of his critics. In that way, too, he was a better scientist than Freud, who tended to be dogmatic. Jung loathed dogmatism, whether it was religious or scientific. In later years he always insisted that he was first and foremost an empiricist. He was always willing to consider evidence.

Jung had been reared in the country whereas most of his fellow students were from town families. Swiss peasants were highly superstitious, as much so as people who were labeled "primitive" in those days. Like most European peasants during the nineteenth century, the Swiss had not been much affected by the intellectual and scientific movements that began with the Renaissance and deepened during the Enlightenment. They were mentally little different from their archaic and medieval forebears. The folklore of their Alemannic ancestors, and earlier prehistoric peoples, still flourished in the countryside. Most of them believed in spirits and ghosts, and practiced folk medicine. The authors of the *Malleus Maleficarum*, which touched off the witch mania of the sixteenth and early seventeenth centuries, found many witches in Switzerland and the Alsace. Archaic pre-Christian beliefs still flourished among the alpine folk during the nineteenth century. Jung had grown up among peasants and fisherfolk in Laufen and Klein-Hüningen, played with their children, and listened to the stories of elders. He was steeped in country lore from his earliest days. It was part of him. Ghosts, spirits, elementals, and magic were familiar to him. As a child, he believed in them.

Years later he wrote in *Memories, Dreams, Reflections*:

> Animals were known to sense beforehand storms and earth-quakes. There were dreams which foresaw the death of certain persons, clocks which stopped at the moment of death, glasses which shattered at the critical moment. All these things had been taken for granted in the world of my childhood. And now I was apparently the only person who had ever heard of them. (Jung 1961, 100)

He put it down to background. After all, he was a country boy. "Plainly the urban world knew nothing about the country world, the real world of mountains, woods, and rivers, of animals and 'God's Thoughts' (plants and crystals)" (Jung 1961, 100).

His mother was probably the most powerful influence of all. Like him, she had a Personality Number Two, as he had discovered in early childhood. She was sometimes strange and mysterious. Something of the pagan past inherited from her Alemannic ancestors lurked behind the conventionally pious, hospitable woman who was not nearly as ordinary as her plump form and bustling housewifely ways suggested. Carl, who knew this other side of his mother, was often mystified when she spoke in her Personality Number Two voice. Then she would make apparently offhand comments that conveyed deep mystery. At times, she seemed to be a ghost, sometimes a witch. Hence, for Carl, the occult was not just something he had read about but which he had experienced firsthand from his earliest childhood. To him it always had been very real.

That reality first dawned with the strange dream of the underground phallus king, which he had never revealed to anyone but which he still remembered and which he still pondered. By the time he was twenty, the dream had taken on added dimensions. He was completely convinced that it had not emerged from anything in his personal experience at the time, nor anything in his innermost personal thoughts, fantasies, or daydreams.

The Jung Medium

In his dissertation, Jung wrote that he participated in seven séances with "S. W." (Helly Preiswerk) between 1899 and 1900. However, according to Stephanie Zumstein-Preiswerk (1975), the séances were held as early as 1895, when Paul Jung was still alive. She states that on an evening in June 1895, six female family members and Jung met at the Klein-Hüningen parsonage for a séance. Among them was young Hélène Preiswerk, whom they called Helly. Born in 1881, Helly had been one of Carl's childhood playmates, probably his first girlfriend. According to Carl, she had a crush on him. Both had the same grandparents: Samuel Preiswerk, who thought he was living in a swarm of spirits, and their grandmother, Augusta Faber, who had been a psychic.

The others at the séances included Helly's mother, Celestine Preiswerk-Allenbach, who disapproved of the séances at first but was finally persuaded; Carl's mother Emilie, who was very enthusiastic about them; Jung's young sister Gertrude (Trudi), and Helly. Jung later referred to Helly as S. W. in his doctoral dissertation, and described her thus:

> S.W. is of delicate build, skull somewhat rachitic though not noticeably hydrocephalic, face rather pale, eyes dark, with a peculiar penetrating look [scarcely the way one would describe one's beloved!]. . . . At school she passed for average, showed little interest, was inattentive. In general, her behavior was rather reserved, but this would suddenly give place to the most exuberant joy and exaltation. Of mediocre intelligence, with no special gifts, neither musical nor fond of books, she prefers handwork or just sitting around day-dreaming. . . . Her educational level was accordingly pretty low and her interests were correspondingly limited. (Jung 1902, par. 38)

One hopes for the sake of Helly's morale that she never saw Jung's description of her. However, it was essential to his thesis. She was neither well read nor philosophically minded. Yet, in trance, she sometimes said things that one might have expected only from someone far more educated and intelligent. This fascinated Jung, and convinced him that there was a hidden mind. This, to be sure, was by no means a new idea, but was the basis of what Ellenberger calls the "First Dynamic

Psychology," by which he means depth psychology based on hypnotism. Jung recognized that Helly's trances were a form of autohypnosis, and this interested him. He did not believe that her spirits were supernatural beings.

At the same time, Jung was persuaded on other grounds that there actually were spirits, and that their reality could be scientifically proven. He was convinced of this chiefly by Zöllner and Crookes, who presented compelling scientific arguments for Spiritism. Jung was also convinced of the reality of psychokinesis (the movement of physical bodies by psychic means). This was because of things that happened during the séances, rather than Helly's usually banal and naive messages from the beyond.

In Spiritualist belief, the medium, as the name indicates, is the intermediary between the natural world and the spirit world, which is very much like this world, but hidden in another dimension and somewhat better. Mediums are very much like shamans, and the Spiritist's "beyond" is very much like that of the typical shaman. The contact on "the other side" is called a control or spirit guide. The control is often a somewhat dramatic figure, a historical character, a composer, novelist, or, in North America, an Indian chief. The control enters the medium's mind unseen and speaks through her voice, hears through her ears, and sees through her eyes. The medium and control form a bridge by which other spirits on "the other side" cross over, and sometimes materialize by manufacturing "ectoplasm." This is a spirit substance that gives the appearance of physical matter. For instance, Samuel Preiswerk once appeared in a white shroud during the Jung–Helly Preiswerk séances. The spirits also make objects move, and cause tables to turn and levitate. In séances conducted by professional mediums, trumpets fly about and horns blow. In Spiritualist belief, the spirits move the planchette about the Ouija board, guiding the hands of those who touch it lightly.

Spiritualism or Spiritism began in 1848 in a small New York town near Rochester. Here, two young girls reported mysterious rappings on the walls. Closer attention indicated that they were in Morse code. According to the Fox sisters, spirits of the dead were communicating with the living by telegraphy. During the late nineteenth century, Spiritualist groups multiplied, and family séances became common both in Europe and in

America. The decline of traditional religion made Spiritualism particularly popular in Europe.

In Jung's time, the British Society of Psychic Research, founded in 1882, was carrying out investigations of such phenomena, and around the turn of the century there was considerable popular interest in them. Here was apparently an empirical proof of life beyond death. By the 1920s, virtually all such occurrences had been found either to have been faked or else to have natural explanations, and interest in parapsychology shifted from mediums to the testing of various forms of extrasensory perception, presumably natural phenomena.

According to Stephanie Zumstein-Preiswerk's book *C. G. Jung's Medium* (1975), Jung was present when it was discovered that Helly was a medium. She describes it thus:

> They gathered around a seventy year old, round, walnut table, an old family heirloom inherited from their grandfather. They put a tumbler of water in the center. Then they touched finger tips to make a circle.
>
> Suddenly the glass began to shake and the table to move. Helly went pale and fell back in her chair, breaking the circle.
>
> "We have a good medium here," said Carl.
>
> What astounded Jung was what Helly said about Nietzsche while in mediumistic trance. Although he was sure that she knew nothing about him in her waking state, she seemed remarkably well informed while in trance. Speaking through her, Samuel supposedly said:
>
> "Carl, Carl, believe your grandfather. Nietzsche's doctrine contains many errors with regard to God." Speaking as if she was the Antiste [Swiss Reformed "bishop"] himself, she counselled Jung to remain faithful to traditional dogma. (Wehr 1988, 72f.)

Sometimes Helly's messages were fancifully embellished with family gossip, romantic tales, and adventures. These were mostly rather banal, and Carl did not find them particularly interesting. For instance:

> Be at peace, my beloved children, and do not be afraid. It is I, your grandfather. And someone else is with me—Carl's grandfather, Professor Jung [Carl Gustav I]. Together we shall watch over you. (Wehr 1988, 72)

One of Jung's clerical uncles tried to stop the séances because he was then preparing Helly for confirmation. Jung, however, insisted on continuing, and had his way. Thereafter, they were held secretly in the Jung home at Bottminger Mill.

By 1899, Helly had less and less success producing convincing psychic phenomena, and indeed, was caught resorting to deception. As he said in *Memories, Dreams, Reflections*, the séances ceased:

> . . . very much to my regret, for I had learned from this example how a No. 2 personality is formed, how it enters into a child's consciousness and finally integrates it into itself. . . .
> All in all, this was the one great experience which wiped out all my earlier philosophy and made it possible for me to achieve a psychological point of view. I had discovered some objective facts about the human psyche. Yet the nature of the experience was such that once again I was unable to speak of it. I knew no one to whom I could have told the whole story. (Jung 1961, 107)

One day during the summer of 1898, Jung witnessed an apparently parapsychological event. He was in his room at the new Jung home at Bottminger Mill, studying. The door was ajar. His mother was knitting in the dining room next to the same walnut table at which the séances were held. Trudi was still at school, and the maid was in the kitchen. Suddenly there was a report like a pistol shot. Jung leaped up and rushed into the dining room. His mother was sitting upright in her armchair, flabbergasted:

"W-w-what's happened? It was right beside me!" she exclaimed. She stared at the table and Jung followed her gaze. The table had split from rim to beyond the center, and not along the join but straight through solid wood. Jung was shocked. He had heard and seen it himself. How could it have happened? The table had dried out for seventy years, and the day was relatively moist for a summer day in Switzerland. There seemed to him to be no plausible explanation.

"Yes, yes," his mother said in her Number Two voice, "That means something" (Jung 1961, 105).

Jung never found a natural explanation. (However, a natural explanation could exist: wood, no matter how well seasoned, can split under changing conditions, and the table had been moved.)

Shortly after this incident, Jung came home around 6 P.M. to find the household in an uproar. There had been another loud report an hour before. It came from the sideboard, a heavy piece of nineteenth-century furniture. They could find nothing. Then Jung opened the cupboard to find that the bread knife had broken into four pieces. The handle was in one corner of the rectangular bread basket, and pieces of blade in the others. The knife had been used for four o'clock tea and then put away. At the time nothing was wrong with it.

The following day, Jung took the shattered knife to one of the cutlers in Basel. The man studied the pieces through a magnifying glass, declared the steel to be sound, and maintained that the knife would have had to have been deliberately broken to produce the result seen.

Jung found no explanation for this incident either. He kept the shattered pieces of the knife, and associates such as Barbara Hannah have seen it. It is still in the possession of the Jung family (Jung 1961, 105f.). Jung wrote Rhine about these experiences in 1934, but the parapsychologist gave no explanation.

In October 1902, Jung visited Helly in Paris, and, in 1905, had her make a dress for his young wife, Emma née Rauschenbach, whom he had married in 1903. Shortly after Emma's death in 1955, Emma appeared in one of Jung's dreams, wearing the dress. "It was perhaps the most beautiful thing she had ever worn," Jung wrote in *Memories, Dreams, Reflections* (1961, 296).

Helly died on November 13, 1911, almost on her thirtieth birthday. Jung named his next-born daughter Hélène in her memory. Jung's doctoral dissertation, based on his experiences with Helly, was *On the Psychology and Pathology of So-Called Occult Phenomena*. His director at Burghölzli, Eugen Bleuler, suggested the topic and supervised it. Jung completed the dissertation in 1902, and it appears in volume I of his *Collected Works*. This dissertation, the Zofingia lectures, and a few excerpts from his diary published by Aniela Jaffé in *Word and Image* are Jung's earliest writings thus far published.

The dissertation is an invitation to look beyond the limits of the exact sciences to what Charles Tart recently called "altered states of consciousness." Jung wrote:

Persons with habitual hallucinations, and also those who are in-spired, exhibit these states; they draw the attention of the crowd to themselves, now as poets or artists, now as saviours, prophets, or founders of new sects. . . .

In view of the—sometimes—great historical significance of such persons, it were much to be wished that we had enough scientific material to give us closer insight into the psychologi-cal development of their peculiarities. (Jung 1902, par. 34–35)

Jung expanded on the theme thus:

The patient pours her own soul into the role of the Clairvoy-ante, seeking to create out of it an ideal of virtue and perfection; she anticipates her own future and embodies in Ivenes [the lead-ing female spirit] what she wishes to be in twenty years' time— the assured, influential, wise, gracious, pious lady. . . . the pa-tient builds up a personality beyond herself. One cannot say that she deludes herself into the higher ideal state, rather she dreams herself into it. (Jung 1902, par. 116)

Jung theorized that the various "spirits" with whom Helly communicated while in trance were actually significant per-sons to whom she had been linked early in her life. These "spirits," he said, were subconscious personalities, repressed thoughts and feelings connected with persons she knew that emerged to lead independent existences of their own as psy-chological entities. Thus:

The individualization of the subconscious is always a great step forward and has enormous suggestive influence on further de-velopment of the automatisms. The formation of unconscious personalities in our case must also be regarded in this light. (Jung 1902, 53f.)

In this very important statement, Jung spoke of the uncon-scious mind for the first time. According to Jung, Helly had several separate personalities whom she gave names such as Ivenes and Grandfather Samuel. These were not spirits in the occult sense, but psychological phenomena that gave rise to her belief in spirits, a point which Jung expanded upon in later years in an essay.

The subconscious personalities seemed very real to Helly, as if physically present, and capable of physical description. For instance, Samuel Preiswerk's spirit appeared clad in white at one of the séances, while Ivenes was a "gracious, pious lady." In a sense they are teleological, as, for example, Ivenes as Helly's idealized self. Perhaps they anticipated Jung's archetypes, some of whom he named: anima, wise old man, the mother, the child, the shadow. However, it is not clear that he had any inkling of the collective unconscious in 1902 when he produced his dissertation. The most interesting of Helly's revelations include a complicated chart, which she described while in a trance. It showed cosmic forces arranged in a configuration of seven concentric circles:

> Outside these there are three more, containing unknown forces midway between force and matter. Matter is found in seven outer circles surrounding the ten inner ones. In the centre stands the Primary Force; this is the original cause of creation and is a spiritual force. (Jung 1902, par. 66)

The whole resembled a mandala. Helly gave Latin-sounding nonsense names to the circles, and concocted a cosmology in which the Primary Force united with matter and gave birth to other spiritual forces. In Helly's cosmology there were two sets of spirits: the somber and pious, and the frivolous and exuberant. As mentioned, Helly was of average intelligence, little education, and, according to Jung, she could not have been capable of such abstruse ideas in a waking state. However, Jung himself gives at least two explanations of where this cosmology came from. On her birthday, he had given her Kerner's *The Seeress of Prevorst*, a popular Spiritualist book. It contained drawings very much like Helly's cosmic mandala. In his dissertation, Jung wrote that he discussed Kant's *Natural History and Theory of the Heavens* in her presence, as well as the law of the conservation of energy, the different forms of energy, and the law of gravity. Knowing Jung's interest in the esoteric, she is almost certain to have produced her diagram to impress him.

It is evident that Jung's interest in Spiritualism and his fascination with split-personality phenomena are entirely consistent with his childhood dreams and fantasies, his preoccupation with Personalities Number One and Two, his manikin in the pencil box, and the concept of shadow. During the 1890s,

Jung probably regarded the unconscious as the psychic substratum of the individual. However, he was familiar with Ernst Haeckel's monism, von Hartmann's metaphysical concept of unconscious mind, and Kant's *Ding an Sich*.

Monism is the concept that reality is a unitary organic whole. Haeckel (1834–1919) was a German zoologist of the University of Jena who loved to coin scientific terms. He invented the terms *ecology* (the study of the relationship between the organism and the environment), *ontology* (the study of embryological development), and *phylogeny*, (a study of evolutionary descent or lineage). His *Generelle Morphologie* (1866) anticipated some of Darwin's concepts in *The Descent of Man* (1871), and, indeed, Darwin said that he would not have written the book had he known Haeckel earlier (Noll 1994, 47f.). German-speaking intellectuals, such as Jung, chiefly learned about biological evolution from Haeckel. He was highly influential. Jung read him during the 1890s without, however, entirely subscribing to some of his more materialistic concepts.

Haeckel coined the phrase "ontogeny recapitulates phylogeny," which he called the Biogenic Law. In this concept, the individual human embryo passes through all of the stages of evolution of the species before birth. Both Darwin and Huxley embraced Haeckel's idea, and, indeed, by the beginning of the twentieth century, it had become axiomatic among the proponents of evolutionary theory. It remains an unresolved issue at the present time. The newborn infant is, biologically speaking, a primitive hominid, according to Haeckel. The Biogenic Law permeated the early schools of child psychology, such as that of Jean Piaget, and occurred in theories as recent as those of Gesell and Ilg during the 1950s.

Jung embraced the theory, and held it to the end of his life. According to Noll, it was the basis of his concept of the collective unconscious. Indeed, Noll speaks of Jung's idea as the "phylogenetic unconscious." I suggest that Jung's theories, such as *Bodenbeschafftenheit*, discussed earlier, and his oft-repeated idea that "We are of immense age," are based on Haeckel. Jung may also have been influenced by Haeckel's *Natural History of Creation* (1868), in which the latter repudiated the Christian concept of a benevolent, loving deity:

If we contemplate the mutual relations between plants and animals (man included), we shall find everywhere and at all times, the very opposite of that kindly and peaceful social life which the goodness of the Creator ought to have prepared for his creatures—we shall rather find everywhere a pitiless, most embittered struggle of all against all. . . . Passion and selfishness . . . is everywhere the motive force of life.

Man . . . forms no exception to the rest of the animal world. . . . The whole history of nations . . . must therefore be [a physio-chemical process] explicable by means of natural selection. (Milner 1990, 208f.)

This idea could have influenced Jung's concept of "God's World," which he claims to have evolved on his own in his boyhood. Did Jung later rework his "boyhood" memories to fit ideas based on Haeckel? It remains possible that, as he said in *Memories, Dreams, Reflections*, he came to the same conclusion as Haeckel on the basis of close observation of natural phenomena such as the warfare of ants.

According to Noll, Jung was also strongly influenced by J. J. Bachofen, a fellow Baseler, whose *Mutterrecht* was widely read and discussed during the 1890s. Bachofen held that there were three main stages in human cultural history: hetairism, matriarchy, and patriarchy. The first stage was characterized by polygamy, polygyny, and wild instinctualism in which both sexes were equal. During the second, matriarchal stage, (*Das Mutterrecht*), Mother Earth was very important, the intellect deemphasized, and agriculture was the basis of the economy. Bachofen called this the Lunar phase. He believed that women invented agriculture during this stage, a view still entertained by some prehistorians, especially feminist archeologists such as Gimbutas. The third stage, symbolized by the sun, is patriarchal. In this Apollonian stage, there was male dominance and glorification of the intellect. Bachofen's ideas were highly influential during the first half of the twentieth century. They complemented Haeckel's Biogenic Law (Noll 1994, 163f.).

In brief, Jung was strongly influenced by the major intellectual currents of the 1890s during his medical school years, which is hardly remarkable. He was impressed by the ideas of Haeckel, Bachofen, Nietzsche, Wagner, and Madame Blavatsky, as well as Zöllner, Crookes, and other specialists in mediumistic Spiritualism. So were many many other educated German-speaking people. He was out of step with other intellectuals in his repudiation of Moleschott, Büchner, and, above all, DuBois-Reymond, whose writings were very widely read and discussed by German-speaking university students during the 1890s. These were all positivists, whose materialism was based on the physics model in science.

From what Jung read, probably did not read, or read and rejected, we can infer his intellectual orientation during his late gymnasium and university years. In most respects, it was typical of the educated classes in the German-speaking countries of the fin de siècle.

All German-speaking people with a gymnasium education were steeped in the Greek and Latin classics as well as German literature. This was the universal norm. German-speaking physicians were frequently very deeply read in the humanities, knowledgeable about music and art, and philosophically minded. Freud and his colleagues, for example, frequently quoted long passages from the Greek and Latin classics from memory. Thanks to their classical education, most Europeans of the nineteenth century who attended gymnasium were better educated than the usual products of North American universities today, many of whom are trained specialists well prepared for the industrial work force or the professions, but who have not been broadly educated. Far from being irrelevant, a classical education produced highly reflective, philosophically minded physicians, lawyers, businessmen, and government officials who had been educated to think critically and exercise their imaginations: who had learned how to learn. They were not technicians like so many of their counterparts today, especially in North America. Most read four or five modern languages with ease as well as Greek and Latin. Today, one would not expect a medical student to spend his Sundays poring over Kant's *Critique of Pure Reason* or devouring von Hartmann's *Philosophy of the Unconscious*. That Jung did so was by no means unusual.

By 1900, Jung was well on the path which led to his doctrine of archetypes of the collective unconscious. He did not actually publish this theory until 1916, when he produced the essay, "On the Psychology of the Unconscious," which can be found in volume 7 of *The Collected Works*. According to Jung, the idea occurred to him in a famous dream, which he had on the return voyage from his trip to the United States that he took in August-September 1909.

In the chapter entitled "Sigmund Freud" in *Memories, Dreams, Reflections*, Jung tells us that in the dream, he descended down through several stories of a house made up of floors decorated in the decor of several eras. Jung (or Jaffé?) embellished this dream, which Jung first revealed to the seminar on analytical psychology in 1925. Inspired by the dream, Jung plunged into a reading program in archaeology, the history of religions, and myth during the autumn of 1909, which led to his writing *Wandlungen und Symbole der Libido* (1912). This book occasioned both the break with Freud and Jung's subsequent development of the concept of collective unconscious.

In summary, our concern here is the origin of Jung's ideas, his intellectual prehistory, so to speak. Jung undoubtedly derived many of his most important ideas from his reading during his gymnasium and university years. At the same time, many of his ideas undoubtedly emerged from childhood and pubertal experiences such as his rambles through the countryside and his close observations of nature. Anyone who observes nature at close range quickly discovers that it is not benevolent, but pitiless, cruel, and highly competitive. Consequently, "God's World," as Jung saw it, did not reveal *agape* or divine love but ruthlessness. The boy did not need Haeckel to tell him that. Because he lived among country people of little education and sophistication, rich in folklore, he did not need Madame Blavatsky or the writers on Spiritualism to tell him about the esoteric and the occult. He had experienced it among the peasants and fishermen of Klein-Hüningen since early childhbood. Even allowing for the unreliability of *Memories, Dreams, Reflections* as autobiography, it is not difficult to account for the childhood origins of many of Jung's most cherished ideas, including the collective unconscious. He may not have articulated it until 1916, but the ultimate origins of the concept in his mind undoubtedly lay in his childhood. With Stern, Homans, and Noll, I think that there are personal explanations for all of Jung's visions and dreams. However, it is apparent that those which he mentions in *Memories, Dreams, Reflections* affected him very profoundly, and were basic to his later conclusions, most of which were worked out between 1909 and 1916 when he was in his thirties. In retrospect, he interpreted his boyhood dreams as breakthroughs of the collective unconscious. Since he undoubtedly had worked over and revised the memories not once but many times by the time he formulated his theories, they were anything but pure childhood recollections. However, they still had enormous impact on his thinking, and to understand how he developed his theory of collective unconscious we have to account for how *he* interpreted them rather than how *we* interpret them.

Six

The Zofingian Papers

In 1900, Jung was clearly on the path that led to the doctrine of archetypes of the collective unconscious. Our earliest available documentary evidences of Jung's youthful thought are in the Zofingian Papers. These were lectures he gave to his fraternity brothers.

The First Zofingian Lecture:
"The Border Zones of Exact Science"

Jung gave his first lecture to Zofingia, "The Border Zones of Exact Science," in November 1896. He was twenty-one. His father was dying of cancer. The family still lived in Klein-Hüningen.

It was a cheeky address, saucy, in fact. ". . . I will introduce you to me," he said. "As many good citizens of Basel here present will gladly testify, my family, on both sides, have always been peculiarly given to offending well-meaning citizens because it is not our custom to mince words and, wearing an amiable smirk, to wheedle our honorable, highly estimable uncles, aunties, and cousins with flattering ways." He warns them: "It would also appear that I was born in an evil hour, for I always speak and behave just as my black heart prompts me to do." As a result, he is guilty of "rudeness," "incivility," "insolence," "cheekiness," and "unmannerliness" (Jung 1896–9, pars. 1, 3). Most of it is youthful hyperbole, no doubt beery talk, but some of it is also authentic Jung as his friends knew him in later years.

In introducing the audience to himself, he took several swipes at the stuffy bourgeois elite of Basel, saying: "I welcome someone to instruct me how to acquire good breeding, and how to walk through the streets like a marionette with a fresh coat of paint on; how much a person has to lie before people will believe he is telling the truth; and how to emulate those virtues, possessed by a titular committee, which shine like beacons before us to show us the way" (Jung 1896–9, par. 7).

After these more or less irrelevant slurs at "elders and betters," which took up about a third of the talk, he finally reached his topic. As in later years, Jung always went round and round topics rather than straight to them, and his anger was never far from the surface.

He began the main body of his talk with a sarcastic attack against the natural sciences of the day and their mechanistic-materialism or positivism:

> As we all know, the principle of inertia is not confined to the field of physical phenomenon but also represents a fundamental law of human thought. As such it is an even more powerful factor in the development of world history than stupidity.
>
> This *principle of inertia*, innate to humankind, permits us to comprehend why nowadays, in the age of the hypercritical mind, we still see educated people in every walk of life—and not least among them physicians and natural scientists—who are not ashamed to proclaim their adherence to materialism, thus bearing witness to their own intellectual poverty. (Jung 1896–9, pars. 13–14)

Jung took his stand on the side of the vitalists, just then under sharp attack, and also with his beloved Kant, whom he frequently quotes, as well as Schopenhauer, to whom he was also devoted. There is no doubt about his philosophical idealism.

The scholarly world, he said, ". . . is like an ocean whose mirror surface remains serene and flawless. Everyone is happy, and people raise each others' spirits by pointing out that everything has been explained and divided into beautiful, orderly, functional compartments." But those who think so "just swim along with the tide." He also attacked the money grubbers and careerists, and the dilettantes. "Do we not have a sacred duty to guard the youthful germ-seed of awakening knowledge from the death-dealing frost of indifference?" He answers, "We

must struggle to gain knowledge. We cannot do otherwise"
(Jung 1896–1899, pars. 20, 38).

> When a nonscientist asks us about the results of the exact sci-
> ences, as a rule we talk—if the field is physics—about the laws
> of gravitation, and about wave and ether theory; in the field of
> chemistry about atomic and molecular theory; in zoology and
> botany about equivocal generation, heredity and natural selec-
> tion; in physiology about mechanism and vitalism. If a scientist
> is honest, he concludes his remarks with a shrug of the shoul-
> ders. But as a rule scientists do not do this, for it looks better to
> pose as an oracle spouting dogmas. It's more impressive. (Jung
> 1896–1899, par. 42)

Physicists speak of gravitation, wave, and ether theories as if
they were "oracles spouting dogmas," and chemists, biolo-
gists, and physiologists do the same in their own fields. They
do it to impress people.

For instance, he said, the theory of evolution traces life back
to the "first cell, rocked by the warm waves of the primordial
sea . . ." What was before it? he challenged his audience. *Omne
vivum ex vivo*. All life comes from life. Logic tips the scale.
"The creation of the first cell must have come about through
contact with preexistent life" (Jung 1896–1899, pars. 56–57).
The *why* lurks in the background, unexplained. "Does that
Ariadne's thread which has led us this far really end abruptly
in the darkness, or does it perhaps continue, leading us out of
the night and into the light?" (Jung 1896–1899, par. 61).

> The position of contemporary sceptical materialist opinion con-
> stitutes, simply, intellectual death. . . . We improve our micro-
> scopes, and every day all they do is to reveal to us new and
> greater complexities. We improve our telescopes, and all they do
> is to show us new worlds and systems. The riddle remains, and
> the only change is that it grows ever more complex. We behold
> the infinity of the world in the microcosm, we behold it in the
> macrocosm. Where does it all end? (Jung 1896–1899, par. 63)

Jung cited examples of hidden and unacknowledged metaphysical thinking from physics and chemistry: theories of
light, molecules, and atoms then current in scientific explanations. "A preexistent vital principle is necessary to explain the

world of organic phenomena" (Jung 1896–1899, par. 63). He concluded: "An immaterial phenomenon that manifests itself only materially: Is that not an irrational claim? Is it not in fact sheer nonsense?" (Jung 1896–1899, par. 65).

In 1904, Albert Einstein demolished the ether theory completely in his special theory of relativity. Today ether is one of many scientific myths, a fairy tale of historical interest, along with phlogiston and Ptolemy's geocentric model of the cosmos. On the other hand, atoms and molecules have been moved from the world of speculation to that of fact, and recent experiments suggest that life can indeed arise from nonlife.

Is science only another form of myth making as Jung seems to suggest? In later years, Jung insisted that he was not a philosopher but an empiricist. Indeed, Franz Jung insisted on this point in a letter to me, as well as in conversation. His father, he said, did not have "concepts," but dealt only in scientifically proven facts. Yet here, in his first Zofingian lecture, Jung confused scientific with metaphysical speculation. In metaphysics, one can speculate forever because, by their very nature, metaphysical propositions cannot be empirically disproven. In science, however, propositions must be verified by testing and are constantly subject to revision, as Thomas Kuhn shows in *The Structure of Scientific Revolutions* (1962). Did Jung ever learn the difference? I suggest that he did not, and that the confusion we find in "The Border Zones of Exact Science" (1896) persisted to the end of his life. To appreciate Jung's insights and ideas, we must, I think, figuratively move him from the faculty of science to the faculty of arts. His contribution has been not to science, but to the humanities.

Jung's interest in his two favorite philosophers, Kant and Schopenhauer, was less in their epistomological discussions than in their excursions into the realm of psychic phenomena. They willingly considered the possibility that there might be spirits, and that they could be communicated with. In *Träume eines Geistersehers Erlautert durch Träume der Metaphysik* (*Dreams of a Spirit Seer Explained Through the Dream of Metaphysics*), Kant explored the empirical possibilities of metaphysical belief, while in *Parerga und Paralipomena*, Schopenhauer wrote: "It is not my vocation to combat the scepticism of ignorance whose cavilling deportment brings it into disrepute every day. Nowadays anyone who doubts the fact of animal magnetism [hypnotism] and the clairvoyance it confers, must not be called sceptical but ignorant" (Jung 1896–1899, par. 76).

Jung's thought in "The Border Zones of Exact Science" shows the influence of Haeckel. It is quite consistent with the latter's monism and vitalism. In 1899, Haeckel published *Die Welträtsel* (*Riddle of the Universe*). It argued that matter and spirit (*Geist*) were one and the same, a concept echoed in Jung's idea of the psychoid archetype, which he arrived at late in life in collaboration with the atomic physicist W. Pauli. Haeckel conceived of the cosmos as an organic unity, hence his philosophical doctrine of monism. All aspects of reality are one. While Haeckel did not publish *Welträtsel* until 1899, as mentioned, his ideas were being widely discussed earlier, during the 1890s, under the name neovitalism. It was an idea that was bound to appeal to a young man who, as a boy, had been so deeply impressed by the dynamics of what he called "God's World." While Jung only mentioned Haeckel in "Thoughts on the Interpretation of Christianity," the fifth and last of his Zofingian lectures, his ideas were probably among those discussed in beery sessions at the Breo by Zofingians. Noll asserts that Jung "read Haeckel copiously," but I am unable to find confirmation of this.

In Haeckel's view, transpersonal divinity permeates every aspect of the phenomenal world: just as in Kant's philosophy, the noumenal is inherent in the phenomenal. I do not see this viewpoint as evidence of *Völkischness* as does Noll, but rather of German idealism. Jung's interest in Haeckel is more evident in *Wandlungen und Symbole der Libido*, published in 1912. According to Noll, Jung was introduced to Eastern philosophy and religion, and astrology, by Toni Wolff, who became his companion in 1911. She, in turn, may have derived these concepts from Blavatsky, whose ideas were highly influential at the time. Much of the interest in the history of religions and the esoteric can be traced to Blavatsky and the Theosophists. As Noll shows, Jung undoubtedly discovered Mithraic mysteries, Max Müller, and solar mysticism and the Germanic mysteries of the *Völkisch* writers while he was engaged in the research for *Wandlungen*, as the bibliography of that work shows. It is problematic how much of it he delved into before then. I think that his knowledge of this line of thought was very superficial and limited until the autumn of 1909. There is little doubt about its impact at that time, as proven by his correspondence with Freud. What I challenge is Noll's overemphasis on *Völkischness*, which is largely based on his classification of almost every trend and development in German intellectual history as a form of that movement. I think that Haeckel influenced Jung more. Above all, we must not underestimate Jung himself, and his own originality of thought.

The Second Zofingian Lecture: "Some Thoughts on Psychology"

Jung began his second Zofingian lecture (1897) with a quotation from Kant, that

> "Morality is always paramount. It is the holy and inviolable thing which we must protect, and it is also the reason and purpose of all our speculations and inquiries. All metaphysical speculations are directed to this end. God and the other world are the sole goal of all our philosophical investigations, and if the concepts of God and the other world had nothing to do with morality, they would be worthless." (Jung 1896–1899, par. 68)

Jung confessed that his last paper nearly had hit the wastepaper basket, but he now wants "to have a chance to walk with you along the Stygian banks to the realm of the shades" (ibid., par. 69). He referred to vitalism, theism, and parapsychology, three topics that he admitted were very unpopular just then among German-speaking intellectuals. His target was Emil DuBois-Reymond, whom he accused of locking doors with "his little key that says 'ignorabimus'" (We will ignore) (ibid. par. 71).

Emil DuBois-Reymond was a professor of physiology at the University of Berlin. He founded the science of electrophysiology and was the first to study electrical activity in nerve and muscle fibers. He collaborated with Hermann von Helmholtz and Carl Ludwig. All three had great impact on biological theory during the late nineteenth century. Their purpose was to found a rigorous scientific physiology on the physics model. Their theories made a deep impression on Freud, whose "Project," written about the same time, was an attempt to construct a psychological system based on Helmholz in particular. Freud and Jung were exposed to this line of scientific theory building at about the same time, and took diametrically opposite positions. Freud embraced it completely. Jung completely rejected it.

Jung's second lecture was an attack against materialism and reductionism. DuBois-Reymond was Jung's *bête noire*. In later years, Jung blamed the death of his father on his problems with theology, suggesting that the distress caused by loss of numinosity might result in cancer. He also argued that no psychological healing was possible without religious faith.

In the introduction to his lecture, Jung attacks "educated philistines" for being "hidebound" (Jung 1896–1899, par. 85). Then, possibly with his recently deceased father in mind, he asks, what is death? What happens when death occurs? The corpse weighs the same as when the person was alive. "The entire organism is there, complete, ready to live, and yet it is dead and we know of no art to make it live again" (Jung 1896–1899, par. 85).

Jung was perplexed. A "strange Something" has vanished. That "Something" was a "vital principle," an elementary force which "in life maintained an accord between the organism and its environment" (ibid., par. 86).

He referred to Kant again:

> It appears that an intellectual being is intimately present with the matter to which it is joined, and that it does not act upon those forces by which the elements relate to each other but rather upon the inner principle of their state. (Jung 1896–1899, par. 86)

There is no such concept in modern psychology, Jung says. He cites Karl Friedrich Burdach (1776–1847), a vitalist, who says that there is sufficient evidence for the immortality of the soul, for, although the reality of the spirit cannot be proven by physics, such tests do not apply because *"the soul must be independent of space and time"* (Jung 1896–1899, par. 98).

Jung agrees, and, by so doing, takes his stand both with the vitalists and the immortalists. He had been reading Johann Zöllner, a leading apologist for Spiritualism, and was deeply impressed. Here Jung reveals his anti-Semitism. "Mortally wounded in his struggle against the *Judaization* [italics mine] of science and society, this high-minded man died in 1882, broken in body and spirit" (Jung 1896–1899, par. 108). His cause was taken up, said Jung, by Wilhelm Weber, a physician who studied electromagnetic induction, and also by the philosopher and psychologist Theodor Fechner. But they were defeated by "the slippery" Carl Ludwig and the "spiteful" DuBois-Reymond "throughout a Germany in moral decline." The so-called Jewish conspiracy triumphed, and DuBois-Reymond, "the Berlin Jew," conquered. "The little group of the faithful melted away" (ibid.).

According to Jung, only Baron Carl DuPrel continued to champion Spiritualism in Germany. In Russia, however, the "noble cause" was championed by Alexander Oksakov, in Austria-Hungary by Julius Wagner, and in Italy by the astronomer Schiaparelli and the anthropologist Lombroso (ibid.).

We have, in this lecture, clear evidence of Jung's youthful anti-Semitism; the earliest, in fact. This charge is denied by Jungians, including Jews closest to Jung, such as Aniela Jaffé. It is a deeply disturbing discovery for those of us who admire Jung, but it can scarcely be denied. Jung, in his youth, clearly identified the materialists as Jews, and spoke of a Jewish conspiracy as well as of the Jewish corruption of German society. This was a negative aspect of *Völkisch* thought. Nearly everyone was a racist in the 1890s, and anti-Semitism, which revived with the Russian pogroms of 1881, was extremely widespread. This stereotype was deeply engraved on the European and American consciousness and was endemic in the culture like an infectious disease.

(Jung was wrong about DuBois-Reymond: he was not a Jew. He was descended from French Huguenots, and boasted of being of "pure Celtic blood." His religious background was Protestant.)

Jung rants on: the materialists (whom he has identified as Jews) have completely triumphed over the idealists. It is as though Kant, Schopenhauer, von Hartmann, and Zöllner had never lived. How he hated materialism! "This loathsome, stinking plant is being grown in all the scientific institutions in the land and well-nourished with the dung of the career men."

Referring to DuBois-Reymond again, Jung said: "a professor drowned in mechanistic psychology" is ". . . sowing the poisonous seed that fecundates confused minds . . ." What is more, "Gradually the mud is seeping down from the heights of the university. The natural consequence is the moral instability of the upper echelons of society and the total brutalization of the working man" (Jung 1896–1899, par. 109).

The clergy, too, were guilty, according to Jung. They contribute to moral decay by their attacks against Spiritualism. They regard it as a materialist conspiracy. Thus, "The worthy educated philistine who believes in nothing he cannot see, blindly places his faith in every anti-spiritualist canard, every wretched lie the journalists tell him, and voluptuously wallows in the quagmire of literature on the subject published by the 'progressive' press" (ibid.).

Jung was twenty-two when he gave this lecture, and von Franz is undoubtedly right when she says that he would not have wanted it published. He would have called it juvenilia, but it is worse. It proves that he was an anti-Semite in his youth. It also shows him in the guise of the "true believer," a fanatic seething with hate. Jung's last Zofingian lecture, given in 1899 when he was twenty-four, is more mature in tone, as we shall see.

Jung had a lifelong hatred of scientific reductionism, while at the same time he insisted that his approach was entirely scientific. He was very well read in philosophy, as indeed, he tells us in *Memories, Dreams, Reflections*. His interest in Spiritualism was twofold. Probably because his father died in his presence during this time, he was fascinated with death. The bereaved frequently become interested in Spiritualism and séances, for both selfish and altruistic reasons. The transition from life to death, in which a living person becomes an inanimate object, is awesome to behold. The thought of one's own death as an inescapable reality is terrifying, even to one who has no belief in future punishment. To Carl Jung, his father's death was pathetic. He died in his early fifties, after an unfulfilled and frustrating life. His only happy years were his student days. His marriage had been unhappy, and he was poorly suited to the ministry. His son grieved for him, not only for his loss of a father, but for the father's own sake. These were all possible reasons for his adopting Spiritualism as a private religion at this time, and for the strident tone of his apologetics. Materialism threatened him personally. Perhaps he was not so much trying to convince his fellow students of the validity of Spiritualism, as to convince himself.

The third of Jung's Zofingian lectures was his presidential address. It is mostly about the Zofingian fraternity itself, and is of no particular interest.

The Fourth Zofingian Lecture: "Thoughts on the Nature and Value of Speculative Inquiry"

Today's neoconservatives with their "bottom-line" rhetoric had their counterparts in the 1890s, an era surprisingly like the 1990s in some ways. Then, as now, those interested in scientific research or scholarship as ends in themselves were constantly assailed by the practically minded, for whom science and philosophy were luxuries. Jung's fourth Zofingian address began with a vigorous *apologia* for science and scholarship that is as relevant today as when he gave it. "Strictly speaking, no science is the least bit useful," he told his fellow Zofingians. It only becomes useful when it "sinks to the level of an industry."

Backward, agrarian Switzerland was becoming industrialized; cities like Basel were growing, and the foundations were being laid of Swiss capitalism in which the gnomes of Zürich were to become the bankers of the world. Jung, who was sometimes reactionary, sometimes conservative, reacted against this change. In this lecture, he rallied to the defense of the scholar, whom the farmer and salesman regard as an idle parasite. "The noblest of all the sciences, philosophy, is now afflicted on a grand scale by that same contempt that has always plagued it on a small scale" (Jung 1896–1899, par. 166). With characteristic anger, Jung said:

> Every industrialist, whether he is a businessman or a factory owner, a chemist or a *physician* [italics mine], judges all endeavors that do not produce tangible results, as useless. (Ibid.)

It is an interesting comment, considering that Jung was a medical student. To his credit, Jung sturdily defended the humanities although he was preparing to enter one of the "useful" professions himself.

He then launched into a particularly fierce assault against materialism, greed, and overweening ambition with all the high-minded moralism of a Dickens or Gladstone. At the same time, much of what he says in this lecture anticipated his *Modern Man in Search of a Soul* many decades later. In this way, there was consistency between Barrel, the medical student, and the older Jung of the 1940s and 1950s.

> Human beings, intoxicated by the pleasures of material success, are throwing themselves into the bustle and tumult of existence. They hope that material success will give them everything. (Ibid.)

Jung traced the modern nation-state, industrialism, and technology to the secularism he deplored. Materialism, he said, is the basis of modern human culture. The church, too, is part of the materialist, secular trend. Jung even includes some of the philosophers whom he otherwise admires among the materialists.

> The concept of secularization of all human concerns has also laid hold on philosophical circles and has found its champions there—for example, Eduard von Hartmann with his immanent and eudaemonistic moral principle. There is also Wilhelm Max Wundt, the advocate of humanistic goals. (Jung 1896–1899, par. 167)

Essentially, Jung protests against modernity. Here we encounter the young man who, as a boy, fancied his Number Two Personality in powdered wig, buckled shoes, and wearing a tricorne hat; the boy who wrote "1786" instead of "1886" on his themes. But this young man was also to become the middle-aged man who built a stone tower at Bollingen, where he prepared meals over an open hearth and where he went up to his bed by candlelight. That man was also steeped in medieval and Renaissance alchemy. In his nostalgia for the medieval, Jung was Gothic in the sense used by early nineteenth-century romantics. He was a kindred spirit to Newman and the Oxford Reformers in England, although he probably was not aware of them; to E. T. Hoffmann, Heine, Novalis, and the other romantic poets and writers of an older Germany. Closer to his own times, he was also one with Wagner and Ludwig I, the mad king of Bavaria, who built medieval castles like Neuschwanstein. Noll lumps all of this into the category of

Völkischness, and, if there is anything to his argument, it is supported most strongly in this particular Zofingian lecture.

On the basis of this lecture, I would put the youthful Jung in the same traditionalist conservative category as the Spanish essayist Ortega y Gasset and T. S. Eliot. These were *real* conservatives. Today, the terms *liberal* and *conservative* have become interchanged. In America, in particular, but also in Europe, the classical liberal of the nineteenth century was devoted to individualism, laissez faire, and the sanctity of private property. Today's "neoconservatives" are really classical liberals. The old, traditional conservatives of the nineteenth century were monarchists, admirers of aristocracy, nostalgic for the medieval, and both romantic and pastoral in outlook. Jung, from boyhood to old age, was of this latter orientation, and his lecture on speculation is a protest against both classical liberalism and Marxist socialism, which he refers to in passing as "social democracy," a misnomer. This lecture is particularly interesting because it was one of Jung's rare excursions into the field of political and social commentary which, for the most part, he avoided, and in which he was noted for naiveté. Like the romantics, his nostalgia was for lands never seen and times never lived. There was never a time in history that even approximated the romantic image of the medieval which Wagner and Jung shared.

Jung's further criticisms include a denunciation of the "pursuit of happiness" as a goal in life. "Thus," he said, "the road to happiness does not lead through the theaters and concert halls, or through honor or glory, but rather up or down into the unfathomable depths of our own being." In this lecture, Jung mentions for the first time the sexual drive, which "frequently transforms man into a monster." As elsewhere, he constantly cited the philosophical works he read each Sunday morning in lieu of going to church: von Hartmann, Schopenhauer, and, above all, Kant. He now mentions Nietzsche, whom he did not read until about then, refers to Schelling in passing, and only mentions Haeckel once and then only to refute him. In general, Noll, Ellenberger, and Mosse attribute Jung's ideas to writers whom Jung never mentions. He always quotes Schopenhauer, Goethe, Kant, and von Hartmann. In his case, I think that neoromanticism, fin de siècle thought, *Bodenbeschafftenheit*, and *Völkischness* were either peripheral to him during his youth, or, and this is more likely, popular ideas in the culture which he picked up at the Breo, the Zofingian meetings, and on other occasions when he talked with his friends. His reading does not seem to have included many of the writers who expounded these ideas. Instead, he seems to have imbibed them more or less subconsciously in the process of working out his own views, so that while his ideas were not original per se, they were original to him.

This lecture is where he shows his religiosity more than elsewhere. From the attack against secularism, he moves to an apologia for religion; not the formal, organized Christianity of the churches, but to an inward-looking personal kind of Christianity akin to that of the Quakers. Jung never mentions the Quakers and does not seem to have been aware of them. However, I think that he would have been very sympathetic to them if he had known them. His own concept of God, from early youth to old age, was very much like the Inner Light, a point which I have made earlier but which is worth repeating here. He was one for whom religion was deeply personal. For him, God was an indisputable, experiential fact, neither a philosophical abstraction nor a theological proposition. He did not *believe* in God, as he so often said in later life, but *knew* He existed.

In this lecture, as in letters to clergymen that Jung wrote late in life, Jung deplores secularism, the loss of medieval man's spiritual vision, and also industrialism, technology, social democracy, and all other characteristics of modernity, much as Ortega y Gasset and Eliot did. To him, as to Eliot, modern culture is a "wasteland." Alienated humanity must recover what has been lost, and this can only be done through religion. Thus, just as he continued to maintain all through his life, Jung stated in this lecture that there is no cure for humanity's ills save through religion. By religion, however, he does not mean the Christian Church of his day, which he considered part of the secular world. Instead, he means something profoundly numinous and personal. It is apparent from this lecture that he was already in the midst of his quest for a new mythology to replace orthodox Christianity.

We place too much trust in this world, we believe too firmly in the happiness to be derived from success, despite the fact that

the greatest of all men, Christ and the sages of all ages, teach
and demonstrate that we should do just the oppposite. (Jung
1896–1899, par. 189)

This lecture is a sermon. Jung is preaching. He says "A person who bases his happiness on things external to himself
may see his whole world crumble overnight" (Jung
1896–1899, par. 190). Everything external to us can change.
His is a very old message, reiterated, as he mentions, not only
by Christ but by the Buddha, Zoroaster, and other founders of
world religions. In my view, Jung had a universal viewpoint
from his earliest years. Perhaps it began in his infancy, when
his mother showed him *Orbis Pictis* with its depiction of
Hindu deities. In retrospect, at least, he claims that he sensed
their numinosity.

Jung eloquently continued in this, his fourth lecture:

Man is a Prometheus who steals lightning from heaven in order
to bring light into the pervasive darkness of the great riddle. He
knows that there is a meaning in nature, that the world con-
ceals a mystery which it is the purpose of his life to discover.
(Jung 1896–1899, par. 194)

And how does he know that? Jung's reply shows how deeply
impressed with Kant he was at that time.

After Plato's problem—the eternal ideas—had fallen, like
Sleeping Beauty, into a sleep that lasted two thousand years,
philosophy, in its manifold transmutations, prepared the way
for the coming of the philosopher of Königsberg, [Kant] . . . [who
raised] the question of the *Ding an sich* [thing-in-itself]. (Jung
1896–1899, par. 195)

The *Ding an sich* eludes perception but is inherent in reality. Science, Jung says, expands our horizons but the *Ding an
sich* lies beyond science. "The absolute realm is not divided
into two distinct realms, the *Ding an sich* on the one hand and
the phenomenal world on the other." No. "All is One" (Jung
1896–1899, par. 197).

Our problem according to Jung is that we separate them:
secularism separates them. Medieval man lived in terms of the
Christian synthesis, an integrated worldview that has been

The Zofingian Papers   153

shattered by modernity. We must transcend the spirit-matter dualism, which the rise of secularism has created. This is a viewpoint that Jung was to expound in greater depth and complexity later in life, especially in his revisions of his theory of the collective unconscious, in which he propounded his theories of synchronicity and the psychoid archetype. The germs of these ideas are to be found in this youthful sermon to his fellow Zofingians. If we repudiate materialism, "the focal point of all concern will shift from the material to the transcendental world." Here, as elsewhere in this lecture, Jung anticipates his later theory of individuation as a plan of salvation, the unity of psyche. He concludes the lecture with a plea, quoted from Nietzsche:

> The earth is losing its gravity, the events and powers of the earth are turning into dreams, and a transfiguration as of summer evenings envelops him. He who beholds this feels as if he were just beginning to wake up, and as if all that remains of the world around him is no more than the vanishing clouds of a dream. In time these too will blow away: for the day has come. (Jung 1896–1899, par. 236)

The Fifth Zofingian Lecture: "Thoughts on the Interpretation of Christianity"

The fifth and last of Jung's five Zofingian lectures was given in January 1899. He was twenty-four at the time. Here, Jung criticized Albrecht Ritschl, a liberal German theologian who was then much in vogue. Ritschl (1822–89), who rejected the mystical element in religion, was the author of *Die Christliche Lehre van der Rechtfertigung und Versohnung* (*The Christian Doctrine of Justification and Atonement*).

Jung objected to Ritschl's rationalism, his emphasis on the historical Jesus, and on his ethical teachings. Jung, in opposition, stressed the numinosity of Jesus as a mysterious figure whose significance transcended rational explanation. "They have not evolved from any historical foundation, but know that in their inmost natures they are free of all contingency. . . ." Christ, in that sense was a "god-man," but not the only "god-man." Buddha was one as well (Jung 1896–99, par. 243).

Jung opened his lecture with a quote from Nietzsche:

A single spark of the fire of justice, fallen into the soul of a learned man, is enough to irradiate, purify, and consume his life and endeavours, so that he no longer has any peace and is forced to abandon forever that tepid or cold frame of mind in which run-of-the-mill savants carry out their daily chores. (Jung 1896–99, par. 243)

There are, however, strange, "almost supramundane beings" who "essentially represent a new species of man." Such figures are the creators of culture. Their values are different from those of the common herd, and they discover new truths.

Since the Renaissance, "Modern people no longer acknowledge the New Testament accounts to be absolutely reliable, but only relatively reliable" (Jung 1896–1899, par. 247). However, this does not justify tossing Christianity out altogether. The rationalists err in measuring Christ by the standards of "normal man." Jung asks whether Jesus is a "normal man" or a "god-man."

It is a rhetorical question. Jung thinks the latter, but what he means by "god-man" is not the usual second person of the trinity. He means rather that Jesus was an extraordinary person.

Jung is perplexed by the spiritual coldness and cerebral detachment of German philosophers and scholars despite their reputation for depth of feeling and sensibility.

How could Kant, who regarded God as a *Ding an sich*, as a "purely negative limiting concept," still have any religion . . .? How can Wundt wax enthusiastic over the ethical purposes of the world, when nothing exists that could achieve or enjoy this purpose? (Jung 1896–1899, par. 248)

These comments are particularly interesting because Jung's earliest glimmerings of the unconscious are often attributed to his reading the German philosophers during his youth, especially Schopenhauer, Kant, and von Hartmann. Yet, having read them with admiration, he is here highly critical of them.

This lecture strengthens Francis Charet's argument that Jung primarily derived his theory of the unconscious from Spiritualism rather than philosophy. His theory did not begin with his reading of Kant, Schopenhauer, and von Hartmann, but with his séances with Helly Preiswerk. These did not convince him of the reality of spooks, but of what Rhine later called "the further reaches of the mind."

Jung's objection to Ritschl is that his "God is compelled to go through official channels whenever he wishes to do something good for man" (Jung 1896–1899, par. 248). What Jung refers to, I think, is Ritschl's reductionism. At heart, Ritschl's deity is a projection of human philosophical categories. He is God made in man's image. Yet, Jung does not go to the opposite side and come to rest in the bosom of Mother Church. Instead, he anticipates his later psychological concepts, which, according to him, are not based on theoretical considerations at all, but on his empirical discovery that the mind is infinitely richer than theology or science conceives.

Jung baffled his fellow students and continued to perplex his closest admirers in later years because of his apparently inconsistent adherence to scientific rationalism at one moment and denunciation of it the next. However, this flowed from a lifelong determination to try all things. Consequently, he staunchly objected to dogmatism and prejudice no matter where he encountered them. This was his chief objection to the orthodox theologians, but also to rationalists like Ritschl.

In Ritschl's theology, Christ is only a moral teacher. Jung notes that the Greeks in antiquity held the image of Theseus or Solon as the model to Athenian youth. The Indians, he said, do the same for the Buddha. Jung at that time obviously knew very little about Indian philosophy and religion (Jung 1896–1899, par. 251).

> The image of the Buddha is drummed into the Hindu boy, or a holy fakir is paraded before him. A boy who reads *Robinson Crusoe* becomes so enthusiastic about the protagonist that his actions are determined by those of his hero, in accordance with that same law of nature that decrees that a black man cannot refrain from wearing the top hat and studs of the European. (Ibid.)

In his criticism of Ritschl, Jung argues that "The compelling character of moral values derives from metaphysics alone, for . . . ethics divorced from metaphysics has no ground to stand on." (A long tradition of humanist philosophy would certainly disagree with this!) According to Jung, "If we view Christ as a [normal] human being, then it makes absolutely no sense to regard him as, in any way, a compelling model for our actions" (ibid.).

The Jesus of the rationalists is a naive idealist, "poor as a church mouse, stripped of his power and glory, and even his keen discernment." Instead, people are turning from church to scientific lectures.

> Modern man must accept the supramundane nature of Christ, no more and no less. If we do not accept it we are no longer Christians, for we are not entitled to bear this name when we have ceased to share the views it implies. . ... We *must* believe even what seems impossible, or we will be abusing the name of Christian. (Jung 1896–1899, par. 287)

Jung's point here is as valid today as it was in 1899. Liberal Christians, even Christian Unitarians, still insist on adopting the mantle of Christianity while denying its essence. Ritschl was guilty of the same attempt to have his cake and eat it too.

Jung first learned all he could from Ritschl, and then became one of his harshest critics. In so doing, he continued to wrestle with the questions raised when, in his imagination, God defecated on Basel cathedral.

The Zofingian Lectures—A Last Word

Today, the reader of Jules Verne's *Twenty Thousand Leagues Under the Sea* or his other pioneer works of science fiction can glimpse the nineteenth-century excitement about scientific progress. We are now jaded, more impressed by the problems of pollution and violence that scientific and technological progress has created than by its achievements. In Jules Verne's stories, the scientist is a missionary, a hero-adventurer, and science itself is a quest. Men are prepared to plunge into the unexplored jungles of South America or to dive into the center of the earth for the sake of Science. Then, to be a scientist was to be the high priest of a cult which promised, ultimately, certainty.

To understand the attitude of Jung, the young medical student, we have to recapture the overheated enthusiasm of the late nineteenth century, and a mindset now wholly alien to us, because scientific optimism was a casualty of Hiroshima. Pollution, the development of ever more destructive weapons of war, and technological unemployment have not necessarily made us unscientific, but they have dampened some of our enthusiasm and weakened our confidence. During the twentieth century, we have witnessed a backlash of unreason as exemplified by the rise of religious fundamentalism and so-called "creation science." Jung's lecture on the limits of science would have found a readier audience at the end of his life than it did when he gave it in 1896. His Zofingian lectures are cautionary. He made them while he was studying science, and he was never disabused of the great value of the scientific method. Built into the scientific method itself is the capacity to be self-correcting. Jung therefore invited his fellow students to test parapsychology. In 1899, at the end of his medical school years, he invited them to take a critical view of Christianity.

In the course of his arguments with his dying father, as well as in his Zofingian lectures, he espoused a philosophy of experiential religion, a kind of personal mysticism which was entirely opposed to doctrinal Christianity, and which repudiated systematic theology. With equal vigor, he also repudiated mechanistic materialism. What is not clear is what he himself believed, perhaps because at this time his ideas were still being worked out. Though couched in the language of reason, emotion seems to predominate in these lectures.

Absent until just before he wrote his state examinations was any suggestion of Jung's later psychological system except as it relates to parapsychology. Here I agree with Francis Charet, who traces the origins of Jung's concept of the unconscious to his Spiritualist experiments with Helly Preiswerk. Jung did so himself in the first of his sixteen lectures on analytical psychology in 1925.

However, in "Student Years" in *Memories, Dreams, Reflections*, Jung tells us that he had at that time no interest in psychiatry; that the psychiatry professor F. Wille bored him; that he had no interest in either psychiatry or psychology until he read the preface to Richard von Krafft-Ebing's *Lehrbuch zur Psychiatrie* during his last year.

The Zofingia lectures show why Jung felt alienated as a university student, misunderstood and unappreciated. Most of his fellow medical students were enthusiastic about science. Jung was, too, but he was painfully aware of what he saw as its limitations. The theological students were keen about Ritschl, whom Jung attacked for his liberalism. However, he also attacked the conservatives. Though claiming to be a scientist, he defended the study of the occult. He championed science, yet he was an implacable foe of the materialism that logically accompanies it.

However, in my view, the inconsistencies are only apparent. By 1900 and the completion of his medical studies, Jung was striving to work out a coherent viewpoint, which he finally achieved by 1916. Attempting to deal with complexity often results in apparent inconsistency; the consistent thinker can be simplistic. This Jung was not, even as a boy. He always saw truth in shades of grey rather than in black and white.

The essence of Jung's youthful philosophy was a synthesis of nature mysticism, parapsychology, and rational empiricism. The most distinct and controversial aspect of his viewpoint was his conviction that the reality of the soul could be scientifically proven. For that reason, he championed parapsychology as a new science with potentiality.

New Directions

During his last year in medical school, Jung was headed for a career in internal medicine, had made a profound impression on the professor of that subject, and was planning to join him in his practice in Munich. However, as he prepared for the state examinations, Jung studied a textbook on psychiatry by Richard von Krafft-Ebing, which completely changed his direction. The preface of this book, which referred to the psychoses as "diseases of the personality," profoundly affected Jung:

> My heart suddenly began to pound. I had to stand up and draw a deep breath. My excitement was intense, for it had become clear to me, in a flash of illumination, that for me the only possible goal was psychiatry. . . . Here at last was the place where the collision of nature and spirit became a reality. (Jung 1961, 108f.)

Jung's friends, as well as his professor of internal medicine, were totally baffled. Why give up such a promising opportunity to become an alienist, a branch of medicine close to being disreputable at that time?

The answer may lie in Jung's comment that medicine had been a compromise for him in the first place. He had really wanted to be an archaeologist and, if not that, a research biologist. Krafft-Ebing's preface revealed to him a field of medicine that dealt with the psyche scientifically. For that reason, he made the drastic and apparently mad decision to abandon both internal medicine and the opportunity for a lucrative practice in order to become a psychiatrist. Unquestionably, it was the right decision for him.

Jung completed his exams successfully, and with only one minor mishap: he missed identifying one of the cultures on one of the microscopic slides. He celebrated by a night at the opera, followed by a brief trip to Munich around Christmas 1900, the last year of the nineteenth century, and then took the train for Basel and a new life (Jung 1961, 110).

Epilogue

C. G. Jung's formative years will always baffle us, because little in *Memories, Dreams, Reflections* can be verified, and there is only one other source (Oeri's). *Memories, Dreams, Reflections* is an old man's highly modified reminiscence; a personal myth, as the author asserts in the prologue. Today, Jung has been subject to considerable deflation in some quarters, and there will be more challenges in future. In that respect, Noll's critique is comparable to Jeffrey Moussaieff Masson's critique of Freud. To be sure, there have been earlier attacks against Jung, but none raise such doubts about him as does Noll's *The Jung Cult*. If Noll is right, the entire tradition of analytical psychology is a fraud, and those of us who have admired Jung have been duped.

Masson called Freud's alleged repudiation of his seduction theory an "assault against truth," and asserted that the "house that Freud built" is exceedingly rickety, having been built on sand. Noll presents a Jung most of us have never met. His Jung was a grandiose, self-deifying charlatan. Nothing he said was original, and, what is worse, the derivative ideas he adopted are worthless.

The least that can be said, according to Noll and Masson, is that Freud and Jung have been grossly overrated and deserve to be consigned to historical oblivion. However, before those of us who admire Freud and Jung wax indignant, we must seriously consider the charges and acknowledge the possibility that Masson and Noll are right. If they are, Freud and Jung are no longer mentors whom we should follow. We then join most contemporary mainstream psychologists and psychiatrists for whom Freud and Jung long ago lost credibility. Outside of their own circles of practitioners and followers, they retain it today only among scholars and students in the field of religious studies, archetypal critics among literary scholars, and some art critics such as Herbert Read. Both Freud and Jung were respected by the late Joseph Campbell and the late Mircea Eliade, but these scholars in the field of mythic studies took a highly critical approach toward them.

Orthodox Freudians and Jungians form relatively closed circles. They read their own journals, attend their own conferences, and have their own institutes where their psychotherapists are trained. In that way, they are like the self-styled "creation scientists" of the Christian Right, who also have their own institutes, conferences, museums, and learned journals. Such considerations are among those which Noll seizes upon in calling analytical psychology a cult. The criticism applies equally well to Freud. For their part, both the psychoanalysts and the analytical psychologists insist that they are scientists, and that Freud and Jung were as well. However, the creation scientists make the same claim.

Biographically speaking, both Freud and Jung began their careers as medical students for reasons of expediency. Neither wanted to be a healer. Both wanted to be archeologists. Both were drawn to biology and, indeed, biology remained the basis of their respective theories. Neither were trained as psychologists, and from their respective beginnings, both were outside the mainstream of the history of psychology. Jung became a psychiatrist at a time when that specialization was rather disreputable and when, indeed, little was known about mental illness. Freud never did become a psychiatrist, but remained a neurologist.

In 1906, Freud and Jung began to correspond after Jung defended Freud from attacks by conservatives in the medical community, and they soon became friends. However, the friendship was based only on correspondence since they were in each other's company very rarely, and only for short periods of time, until late August 1909. Jung was at first skeptical of Freud's sexual theory of libido. Later, he embraced it, but probably still had reservations. Between 1906 and August 1909, Freud and Jung had a kind of father-son relationship, during which time Jung became a practicing psychoanalyst.

Both Freud and Jung did scientific medical research, which they published in reputable journals until the late summer of 1909. This is generally acknowledged. In late August and early September of that year, both Freud and Jung, as well as their colleague Sandor Ferenczi, spent seven weeks together on a trip to America, where they lectured at Clark University in Worcester, Massachusetts. This trip, in my view, was the most crucial single event in the lives of both Freud and Jung. This is not because of anything that happened in America, but because of what occurred between them on shipboard during the crossings, and what they did after their return to Europe as a result of this.

Until the autumn of 1909, their interests had been medical and their research clinical. Psychoanalysis was a form of psychotherapy for the treatment of neurosis from the early 1890s, when Josef Breuer and Freud invented the technique, until October 1909. After his return to Switzerland from America, Jung plunged into an ambitious reading program in mythology which, as Noll tells us, was a collaborative effort. Jung also set assigned research tasks and reading assignments to young assistants, such as Sabina Spielrein and Johann Honegger. The latter were on the staff of Burghölzli Mental Hospital, where Jung had been employed until 1907, when he went into private practice in the village of Küsnacht near Zürich. This research led to the writing and publication of *Wandlungen und Symbole der Libido*, which appeared in completed form in 1912.

During the autumn of 1909, Jung also inspired Freud to psychoanalyze culture, which led first to his biographical study of Leonardo da Vinci, and then to *Totem und Tabu* (1913), an essay on the origins of religion. Needless to say, Jung found little to agree with in the latter.

Between September 1909 and early 1911, relations between Freud and Jung became strained. In part, this was because of a clash in temperament, and in part because of profound differences in ideas. Jung became impatient with Freud's overbearing paternalism and dogmatism; Freud, on his part, became increasingly alarmed by Jung's enthusiasm for myth, mysticism, and the occult. These were among among the many incompatibilities that led to the final separation. In 1912, Jung made a trip to America, where he lectured at Fordham University. Here, he openly repudiated Freud's sexual theories. At about the same time, Part II of *Wandlungen* appeared, in which Jung rejected Freud's theories in the last chapter, "The Sacrifice." Later, at a conference in Munich, the two men took a long walk together and patched up their differences. Soon after, the relationship again fell apart, and in January 1913 they broke off their friendship.

By this time, Freud and Jung had become bitter foes. As well, psychoanalysis had ceased to be a purely medical psychotherapeutic technique (although it claimed to retain that function), but had become a kind of philosophical or social movement. During the years 1913–20, Jung founded analytical psychology, a movement of his own, which from the start had many of the characteristics of a religious cult. From then on to the present day, the histories of both psychoanalysis and analytical psychology have been of great interest to cultural historians and students of the history of religion.

Masson and Noll, who have been among those who have brought the nonscientific aspects of psychoanalysis and analytical psychology to our attention, have attempted to demolish psychodynamic psychology. They do so on the basis of very erudite scholarship, which is, however, flawed by their obvious bias. Neither are objective in tone, or in the way that they marshal their facts. Instead, both present polemics. In consequence, not only must we be skeptical of Freud and Jung, but of their detractors as well.

I think that Jung was a Dionysian philosopher, like Nietzsche, whose concepts were basically nonrational if not irrational, and who delights romantics such as myself at the same time that he infuriates rationalists. If logic is necessary to the definition of philosophy, then Jung is not a philosopher, but if it is not essential, then he is. Or, was Jung the founder of a religion, as Stern and Noll claim—a failed prophet, as Stern asserts? Jung certainly didn't see himself this way. He always insisted that he was an empiricist. Since individuation could be considered a plan of salvation, there is a sense in which Noll is right in calling him the founder of a charismatic movement. To some, though by no means all admirers of Jung, he was that. I think that he always *will* be an enigma—more so than Freud.

As I have insisted at the outset of this study, and repeated throughout, we know almost nothing about Jung's boyhood because *Memories, Dreams, Reflections* is notoriously unreliable. What we have is a myth, and Noll appropriately begins with a "quest for the historical Jung." He says that *Memories, Dreams, Reflections* tells us more about Jaffé, who wrote most of it, than it does about Jung. I have my doubts about this. I was impressed by her candor and honesty. However, she was also obviously devoted to him, and loyal to his memory. I disagree with Noll's assertion that Jung was deliberately deceptive and manipulative. I also think that he carries the argument that Jung engaged in self-deification much too far. After attending one of the last Eranos sessions at Ascona, where I talked to a number of people who had known Jung personally, I do not believe that Jung deliberately set out to found a charismatic cult. Instead, as I have mentioned but must repeat, one seems to have grown up around him.

One of the discoveries that many readers of *Memories, Dreams, Reflections* makes is how Jung's mature concepts emerged from early childhood experiences. Whatever that enigmatic dream of the underground phallus king actually meant, it impressed him very deeply. I do not agree with his far-fetched etymological and mythical interpretations of it, which he worked out around 1927, long after the dream itself, but I have no doubt that this dream both haunted and puzzled him. Whatever it was, it marked the beginning. What followed were a series of dreams and visions which, in retrospect, the middle-aged Jung used as building blocks for his theories. His employment of "imaginative thinking" in interpreting childhood dreams and visions gave him what he regarded as vital insights.

Whether Jung's dreams, fantasies, and visions had a pathological component, they are the ultimate source of his theory of the collective unconscious. I do not think that he proved the existence of the collective unconscious empirically, or that it has been proven since his time. Nor do I think that those who regard dreams as meaningless brainstorms have *disproved* the significance of dreams. It has been proven that if we do *not* dream, there are psychotic consequences. Beyond that, we still do not know if the dream is the royal road to the unconscious or, indeed, if there actually *is* an unconscious, or if there is a collective unconscious. Other explanations of the diffusion of mythic and dream motifs exist besides Jung's.

Noll underestimates Jung's personal contribution to our understanding of humanity. He developed a system that he called analytical psychology, based on the thesis that there is a universal, impersonal dimension of psyche. This theory had antecedents, especially in German romanticism and certain late nineteenth-century intellectual movements that arose from German romanticism. As such, analytical psychology is an important facet of German intellectual history. It has had considerable impact on a number of writers, artists, social theorists, and historians of religion. What is more, it is also bound up with a system of psychotherapy that has been effective with some patients though not with others. This much is on solid ground. Almost everything else is a matter of speculation.

Positively speaking, I think that both Freud and Jung had certain valuable insights into the nature of culture. The fact that they remain unproven is not to say that such insights are worthless. There is actually some evidence for the collective unconscious. It is far from conclusive, and it is open to debate. The same is true of Freud's theory of the personal unconscious, as Jung always acknowledged. B. F. Skinner's behavioristic theories may be empirically rigorous, but their scope is severely limited, leaving out much in the human experience that is of vital concern. In my view, psychology is a soft science, with few proven facts and many theories. It is possible to classify many of the more than forty schools of psychotherapy as religious cults.

Having said that, it must be emphasized that the scientific method is just that. Science is not so much a body of knowledge as a way to discover truth. The essence of the scientific method is empirical verification. The good scientist gathers data, formulates hypotheses, and subjects them not only to his or her own validation but to those of other scientists.

As I have already stated, Jung started out as a scientist. His dissertation is a competent, objective study; by no means flawless, to be sure, but nonetheless balanced and rational. The same was true of his early psychiatric papers. His *On Dementia Praecox* (1904), which won Freud's praise, was a solid clinical study. The first volume of *Collected Works* contains a number of psychiatric papers that won Jung well-deserved recognition. Had he continued in this vein, he might have built a solidly scientific psychiatric career.

Because he was mentally unstable, perhaps even psychotic at times, Jung plunged instead into the wilder fields of the occult and mythology. Much of his writing is incomprehensible, inconsistent, and illogical. However, his theory of the collective unconscious has caught the imagination of millions of people throughout the world.

As the novelist J. B. Priestley once said to me, "He was the greatest great man I have ever met."

Bibliography

A great deal has been written and published about C. G. Jung, most of it during the 1970s, around the centennial of his birth in 1875. The literature falls into two major categories. The first consists of studies and memoirs by analysts, especially those who knew Jung well and were his associates. The authors include Barbara Hannah, Marie-Louise von Franz, Laurens Van der Post, Joseph Henderson, Edward Whitmont, Edward Edinger, and, above all, Aniela Jaffé, Jung's secretary during his last years. The second category is made up of critical studies that also appeared during the 1970s and early 1980s. The harshest of these is Paul Stern's; the most useful, in my view, is Peter Homan's *Jung in Context*. Among the most recent is Richard Noll's *The Jung Cult*. It is important to study both the apologists for Jung and the critics, and I have done so in the course of my research.

The sources for all studies of Jung remain the eighteen volumes of his *Collected Works*, his published correspondence in the two volumes of *Letters*, as well as the invaluable *Freud/Jung Letters* edited by William McGuire. Although there is a vast library of published work on Jung, there is still much to come as scholars continue to mine the rich treasury of Jungian literature. During the late 1980s and 1990s, specialized studies have appeared, such as *C. G. Jung's Psychology of Religion and Synchronicity* (1990) by Robert Aziz and Francis Xavier Charet's *Spiritualism and the Foundations of C. G. Jung's Psychology* (1993) as well as Harold Coward's *Jung and Eastern Thought* (1985) and Noll's *The Jung Cult* (1994). Henri Ellenberger's *Discovery of the Unconscious*

(1970), though older, remains one of the best studies in the field.

In the course of my reading, certain studies have been particularly helpful. They include the following:

Adler, G. 1964. The memoirs of C. G. Jung. In *Spring*.

Aziz, R. 1990. *C. G. Jung's Psychology of Religion and Synchronicity*. Albany: State University Press of New York.

Baumannn-Jung, G. 1975. Some reflections on the heritage of C. G. Jung. In *Spring*.

Brome, V. 1978. *Jung: Man and Myth*. London: MacMillan.

Charet, F. X. 1993. *Spiritualism and the Foundations of C. G. Jung's Psychology*. Albany: State University Press of New York.

Franz, M.-L. von. 1976. *Jung: His Myth in Our Time*. London: Hodder and Stoughton.

Hannah, B. 1976. *Jung: His Life and Work: A Biographical Memoir*. New York: G. P. Putnam's Sons.

Homans, P. 1979. *Jung in Context: Modernity and the Making of a Psychology*. Chicago: The University of Chicago Press.

Howells, A. 1987. *Jung's Symbolism in Astrology*. Wheaton, Ill.: The Theosophical Publishing House.

Jacobi, J. 1959. *Complex/Archetype/Symbol*. Princeton, N.J.: Princeton University Press.

Jaffé, A. ed. 1979. *C. G. Jung, Word and Image*. Bollingen Series XCVII:2. Princeton, N.J.: Princeton University Press.

_____. 1984. Details About C. G. Jung's Family. In *Spring*.

Jung, C. G. 1896–1899. *The Zofingia Lectures (1896–1899)*. William McGuire, ed. Jan Van Heurch, trans. Bollingen Series XX. In *CW*, supplementary vol. A. Princeton, N.J.: Princeton University Press, 1983.

_____. 1906–1961. *Letters*. Gerhard Adler and Aniela Jaffé, eds. R.F.C. Hull, trans. 2 vols. Princeton, N.J.: Princeton University Press. 1973–1975.

_____. 1961. *Memories, Dreams, Reflections*. Aniela Jaffé, ed. Richard and Clara Winston, trans. New York: Vintage Books, 1973.

Looser, G. 1966. C. G. Jung's childhood prayer. In *Spring*.

Mosse, G. L. 1981. *The Crisis of German Ideology: Intellectual Origins of the Third Reich*. New York: Howard Fertig.

Murray's Handbook for Travellers in Switzerland, 1838. New York: Humanities Press, 1970.

Noll, R. 1994. *The Jung Cult: Origins of a Charismatic Movement.* Princeton, N.J.: Princeton University Press.

Oechli, W. 1922. *History of Switzerland, 1499–1914.* Cambridge: The Cambridge University Press.

Oeri, A. 1970. Some youthful memories of C. G. Jung. In *Spring.*

Stern, P. J. *C. G. Jung: The Haunted Prophet.* New York: George Braziller.

Van der Post, L. 1978. *Jung and the Story of Our Times.* London: Penguin Books.

Wehr, G. 1988. *Jung: A Biography.* David M. Weeks, tr. Boston: Shambhala.

Zumstein-Preiswerk, S. 1975. *C .G. Jung's Medium.* Munich: Kindler Verlag.

A complete listing of references cited follows on page 173.

References Cited

Adler, G. 1964. The memoirs of C. G. Jung. In *Spring.*

Aziz, R. 1990. *C. G. Jung's Psychology of Religion and Synchronicity.* Albany: State University Press of New York.

Baumannn-Jung, G. 1975. Some reflections on the heritage of C. G. Jung. In *Spring.*

_____. 1975. Some reflections on the horoscope of C. G. Jung. In *Spring.*

Brome, V. 1978. *Jung: Man and Myth.* London: MacMillan.

Charet, F. X. 1993. *Spiritualism and the Foundations of C. G. Jung's Psychology.* Albany: State University Press of New York.

Eliade, M. 1963. *Patterns in Comparitive Religion.* Cleveland: World Publishing Company.

Ellenberger, H. 1970. *The Discovery of the Unconscious: The History and Evolution of Psychodynamic Psychiatry.* New York: Basic Books.

Franz, M.-L. von. 1976. *Jung: His Myth in Our Time.* London: Hodder and Stoughton.

Hannah, B. 1976. *Jung: His Life and Work: A Biographical Memoir.* New York: G. P. Putnam's Sons.

Homans, P. 1979. *Jung in Context.* Chicago: The University of Chicago Press.

Howells, A. 1987. *Jung's Symbolism in Astrology.* Wheaton, Ill.: The Theosophical Publishing House.

Hugger, P. 1984. *Kleinhüningen.* Basel: Birkhauser Verlag.

Jacobi, J. 1959. *Complex/Archetype/Symbol.* Princeton, N.J.: Princeton University Press.

Jaffé, A. 1972. The creative phases in Jung's life. In *Spring.*

_____, ed. 1979. *C. G. Jung: Word and Image*. Bollingen Series XCVII:2. Princeton, N.J.: Princeton University Press.

_____. 1984. Details about C. G. Jung's family. In *Spring*.

Jung, C. G. 1896–1899. *The Zofingia Lectures (1896–1899)*. Bollingen Series XX. In *CW*, supplementary vol. A. Princeton, N.J.: Princeton University Press, 1983.

_____. 1902. On the psychology and pathology of so-called occult phenomena. In *CW*, vol. 1. Princeton, N.J.: Princeton University Press, 1970.

_____. 1906–1961. *Letters of C. G. Jung*. R.F.C. Hull, trans. 2 vols. London: Routledge and Kegan Paul, 1974.

_____. 1907. The psychology of dementia praecox. In *CW*, vol. 3. Princeton, N.J.: Princeton University Press, 1960.

_____. 1916. The structure of the unconscious. In appendices to *Two Essays on Analytical Psychology*. In *CW*, vol. 7. Princeton, N.J.: Princeton University Press, 1953.

_____. 1917. On the psychology of the unconscious. In *CW*, vol. 7. Princeton, N.J.: Princeton University Press, 1953.

_____. 1919. Instinct and the unconscious. In *CW*, vol. 8. Princeton, N.J.: Princeton University Press, 1960.

_____. 1925. *Analytical Psychology: Notes of the Seminar Given in 1925 by C. G. Jung*. William McGuire, ed. Bollingen Series XCIX. Princeton, N.J.: Princeton University Press, 1989.

_____. 1939. Conscious, unconscious, and individuation. In *CW*, vol. 9i. Princeton, N.J.: Princeton University Press, 1959.

_____. 1952. Synchronicity: An acausal connecting principle. In *CW*, vol. 8. Princeton, N.J.: Princeton University Press, 1960.

_____. 1954a. Archetypes of the collective unconscious. In *CW*, vol. 9i. Princeton, N.J.: Princeton University Press, 1959.

_____. 1954b. The structure of the psyche. In *CW*, vol. 8. Princeton, N.J.: Princeton University Press, 1960.

_____. 1954c. Psychological aspects of the mother archetype. In *CW*, vol. 9i. Princeton, N.J.: Princeton University Press, 1959.

_____. 1961. *Memories, Dreams, Reflections*. Aniela Jaffé, ed. Richard and Clara Winston, trans. New York: Vintage Books, 1973.

Leibbrand, W. 1954. Schellings Bedeutung fur die Moderne Medizin. Alti del XIV Congresso Internationale di Storia della Medicine. Rome.

Looser, G. 1966. C. G. Jung's childhood prayer. In *Spring*.

Milner, R. 1990. *The Encyclopedia of Evolution*. New York: Henry Holt.

Mosse, G. L. 1981. *The Crisis of German Ideology: Intellectual Origins of the Third Reich*. New York: Howard Fertig.

Murray's Handbook for Travellers in Switzerland, 1838. New York: Humanities Press, 1970.

Noll, R. 1994. *The Jung Cult: Origins of a Charismatic Movement*. Princeton, N.J.: Princeton University Press.

Oechli, W. 1922. *History of Switzerland, 1499–1914*. Cambridge: The Cambridge University Press.

Oeri, A. 1970. Some Youthful Memories of C. G. Jung. In *Spring*. Smith, W. D. 1991. *Politics and the Sciences of Culture in Germany 1840–1970*. New York: Oxford University Press.

Stern, P. J. 1979. *C. G. Jung: The Haunted Prophet*. New York: George Braziller.

Van der Post, L. 1978. *Jung and the Story of Our Times*. London: Penguin Books.

Wehr, G. 1988. *Jung: A Biography*. David M. Weeks, tr. Boston: Shambhala.

Zumstein-Preiswerk, S. 1975. *C .G. Jung's Medium*. Munich: Kindler Verlag.

Index

Index 181

V
Van der Post, Laurens, 13, 42,
   56–60, 62, 66
Vitalism, 18, 140
Von Franz, Marie-Louise, 3, 5,
   13, 32, 59, 72, 105
Völkerpsychologie 47–48
Völkischness, 18, 29, 35, 41–45,
   47, 60

W
Waidling (gondola), young Carl
   and the, 95
Water archetype, 61.
*Wandlungen und Symbole der
   Libido,* 35

Wehr, Gerhard, biographer, 13
Wilhelm, Richard, introduces
   Jung to Chinese mysticism,
   57
"Wise Old Man," 119
Wolff, Antonia (Toni), 37
Wotan, 55
Wundt, Wilhelm, 48

Z
Zofingians, activities of, 32, 47,
   111, 118–19
Zofingia, founding of, 32, 118
Zofingia, papers, 14, 32, 45,
   120–121